Fragrant Offerings

Other Crossway Books
by Debra Evans

The Mystery of Womanhood

Heart and Home

The Expressions of Womanhood Series
Beauty for Ashes
Fragrant Offerings

Fragrant Offerings

DEBRA EVANS

CROSSWAY BOOKS
Westchester, Illinois
A DIVISION OF GOOD NEWS PUBLISHERS

*With special thanks to Judith Markham, Karen Mulder
Lane Dennis and David Evans.*

Fragrant Offerings © 1988 by Debra Evans.

Published by Crossway Books, a division of
Good News Publishers, Westchester, Illinois 60153.

Book and cover design by Karen L. Mulder.
Illustrations by Mark Marcuson.

First printing, 1988

Printed in the United States of America

Library of Congress Catalog Card Number 88-70696

ISBN 0-89107-500-3

For my friend and sister in Christ,
Rogene Argue,
whose fragrant offerings
have touched our hearts with love

Contents

INTRODUCTION ix

PART I   REFLECTIONS ON BEING A BELIEVER
  Chapter 1   Becoming 17
  Chapter 2   Choosing 27
  Chapter 3   Turning 37
  Chapter 4   Walking 47

PART II   REFLECTIONS ON ABIDING IN CHRIST
  Chapter 5   Abiding 61
  Chapter 6   Seeking 71
  Chapter 7   Praying 83
  Chapter 8   Praising 95

PART III   REFLECTIONS ON SERVING GOD
  Chapter 9   Sharing 109
  Chapter 10   Serving 121
  Chapter 11   Laboring 131
  Chapter 12   Proclaiming 141

SUMMARY   REACHING 151

BIBLIOGRAPHY 157

Introduction

> God intends the Christian life to be
> a life of joy, not drudgery. In fact,
> just the opposite is true. Only those
> who walk in holiness can experience true
> joy.
> —JERRY BRIDGES

For today's woman, the promise found in 1 Peter 1:8 is a welcome and refreshing one. There God tells us that those who love and believe in Him will be "filled with an inexpressible and glorious joy." Or, as Jerry Bridges puts it: the Christian life is joy, not drudgery. There are many days when we—as individuals and as women—need to claim and cling to that promise.

In *Fragrant Offerings* I share insights from my own life and the lives of other believers regarding this joy-filled life, and I examine how we, as women, can express this joy daily. My purpose in doing this is to encourage you to reflect on your own walk with the Master, to compare it to the women of His day, and to begin to see that walk as the ultimate expression of your womanhood—all that God has created you to be.

Walking with the Lord is a costly commitment that needs strengthening daily through Bible study, prayer, and quiet meditation. But time is at a premium in our unquiet lives. Therefore, I have tried to help and encourage you to study, pray, and meditate by drawing sources for reflection together into this slender, handy volume.

Fragrant Offerings is designed to let you draw upon the valuable resources that are ours—and what a rich heritage it is! Biblical accounts of women who put their faith in God; a treasury of 150 Psalms; classical literature written over centuries of Christian experience, reflected in the lives of the saints; and devotional literature from more recent times.

In the following chapters you will find a collection of themes to consider as you set aside quiet moments to examine your own faith and, in doing so, to build your faith. The heart of each chapter focuses on a woman from Scripture who reflects the topic under discussion. Along with this, there are my personal comments and reflections; a selection of quotations from the Scriptures and from other believers; ideas for putting principles into practice; open-ended questions to prompt your own self-examination; and suggestions of specific Psalms and verses for personal Bible study.

Keep a journal of your thoughts and reactions to what you read and discover. Be absolutely honest, and you will have a lasting record to refer to in the future. Some space has been provided for personal notes within the book itself, but you will probably want to keep a notebook (a plain, lined, spiral-bound one works great).

There are no cookbook recipes or foolproof formulas that can turn us instantly into mature women of God. It takes time, but the rewards are eternal. Are you willing to risk making the investment? Are you ready to be surprised by what the Lord can do?

"Jesus rarely comes when we expect Him; He appears where we least expect Him, and always in the most illogical connections. The only way a worker can keep true to God is by being ready for the Lord's surprise visits," wrote Oswald Chambers. "It is not service that matters, but intense spiritual reality, expecting Jesus Christ at every turn. This will give our life the attitude of child-wonder which He wants it to have." As you read this book and take time to savor the sweet fragrance of His love, my prayer is that you will find the Lord often waiting to surprise you.

> May the God of hope fill you with
> all joy and peace as you trust in
> him, so that you may overflow with
> hope by the power of the Holy Spirit.
> — ROMANS 15:13

PART ONE

Reflections on Being a Believer

Be imitators of God, therefore,
as dearly loved children
and live a life of love, just as Christ loved us
and gave himself up as a fragrant offering
and sacrifice to God.
— EPHESIANS 5:1-2

Take My Life

Take my life, and let it be
Consecrated, Lord, to Thee.
Take my moments and my days;
Let them flow in ceaseless praise.

Take my hands, and let them move
At the impulse of Thy love.
Take my feet, and let them be
Swift and beautiful for Thee.

Take my voice, and let me sing
Always, only, for my King.
Take my lips, and let them be
Filled with messages for Thee.

Take my silver and my gold;
Not a mite would I withhold.
Take my intellect, and use
Every power as Thou choose.

Take my will, and make it Thine;
It shall be no longer mine.
Take my heart, it is Thine own;
It shall be Thy royal throne.

Take my love, my Lord, I pour
At Thy feet its treasure-store.
Take myself, and I will be
Ever, only, all for Thee.

—FRANCES RIDLEY HAVERGAL
1836-1879

Becoming

Then Mary took about a pint of pure nard, an expensive perfume; she poured it on Jesus' feet and wiped his feet with her hair. And the house was filled with the fragrance of the perfume.
—JOHN 12:3

*Those who are God's are always glad,
when they are not divided, because they
only want what God wants, and want to
do for him all he wishes. Peace of con-
science, liberty of heart...freedom from the
fears and the insatiable desires of the times
multiply a hundredfold the happiness
which the children of God possess...if they
are faithful.*
> — FRANCOIS FENELON
> 1651-1715

*I was not born free.
I was born to adore and obey.*
> —C.S. LEWIS
> 1898-1963

A dozen women's magazines line the checkout counter at the grocery store, each cover announcing the latest formula for being a sex symbol, a super mom, or a career success. Impulsively we slip one or two magazines into the cart, hoping we've at last found the secret that will make us as slim, beautiful, assertive, or competent as we would like to be—or think we should be. The pictures are so bright, the people so appealing, it's hard not to believe them.

We're doomed to disappointment, of course. For once home, settled down in a comfortable chair with a cup of tea, we look inside the glossy cover and discover that the articles and ads are only promoting a new deodorant or beauty aid, or rehashing advice we've heard a hundred times before.

If we hope to achieve anything "significant," the headlines say—implicitly or explicitly, we must meet certain expectations, adopt certain values and attitudes. We must be out there aggressively fighting and winning, whether it means conquering fat, keeping a mate, or intimidating the boss. Most of this advice contradicts Jesus' teachings; yet even within our churches there are many who urge us to heed these voices of the culture rather than the call of the Master.

"The kingdom of God," writes Charles Colson, "is a kingdom of paradox, where through the ugly defeat of the cross a holy God is utterly glorified. Victory comes through defeat; healing through brokenness; finding self through losing self."

This means that the things of this world—the bent of our culture—are at war with the kingdom of Jesus Christ. Until we realize this and recognize the scope of the battle and clearly align ourselves with Christ and His kingdom, we will not be able to serve Him with singleness of heart. But when we do, as women who have been redeemed, forgiven, and accepted in all of our individual uniqueness by our heavenly Father, we no longer need to fear the opinions of others or these pressures of society.

"Our sense of identity is found first by looking to God from our innermost selves and letting all of our roles, feelings, attitudes, and relationships find themselves in relation to him," says L'Abri director Dick Keyes. In being restored to their true identity by being reconciled to their personal Creator, he says, men and women can discover real freedom.

Our self-worth is based on God's view of us, not on our own opinions or others' attitudes toward us. Our identity is centered in the reality of what Jesus has accomplished on our behalf.

As you read the following poem, consider Mary of Bethany's disregard for the opinions of others. How would people today react to her expression of love for Jesus? And why is the Lord's response to Mary so startling—and so liberating?

❦   ❦   ❦   ❦   ❦

No one could have guessed what she was
about to do:
     Ignoring the guests at the dinner party,
     She poured out the contents of her heart
     freely.
In one quick motion she shattered
   the jar she carried;
Chips of alabaster sprinkled the hem of her
   brightly colored dress.
     The fragrance of the nard
     Hit each witness full force—
     It was a distinctly unforgettable odor,
     Reminiscent of funeral processions.
Outraged, Judas asked,
    "Why this waste?"
    This perfume could have been sold
    At a high price and the money given away
    To the poor!"
Amidst the murmuring group,
The woman was aware of Jesus only;
Nothing else she had ever done
Compared to this act of love.
And then He said:
    "Leave her alone.
    Why are you bothering her?

She has done a beautiful thing to Me."
Soon afterward, Judas left with a plan
To betray Jesus for thirty pieces of silver.

Let us remember this woman
At our Savior's request—
We can choose to be like her
Regardless of our critics.

In spite of what others may think,
We will always be welcome
At the feet of the Master.

❦   ❦   ❦   ❦   ❦

Considering the Challenge
"Why this waste?"

Has anyone ever asked you why you are "wasting" your time or talents on being a Christian? Have you ever asked yourself the same question?

Just as you are ready to walk out the door, the phone rings. It's someone from church who needs to talk to you about her latest family crisis. You listen halfheartedly, fingering your car keys and thinking, *Why am I wasting my time talking to her about these problems? No matter what I say, she's still going to keep right on messing up her life. What a waste of time! I could be halfway to the store by now. At this rate, dinner will be delayed at least thirty minutes.*

When we begin considering how our lives might be better spent, self-doubt creeps in. The mother of a colicky baby worries about what's become of her life as she paces the floor at three in the morning. *What about my needs and desires? All my artistic talent is going right down the drain; between changing diapers and holding a fussy baby, there's never enough time for painting. Whatever happened to the energetic, creative young art student I used to be?*

A single woman in her late twenties wonders whether she has missed her opportunities for love. While working on a special church project far from home, she pictures the husband and children she has always wanted. *Other women I know have had no difficulty finding men with whom they could share their futures. Am I really where You want me to be, Lord? I feel as if I will be missing the best moments of my life if I continue to fulfill my commitment to this job. Is this ministry really worth it all?*

Following Jesus in the midst of life as it actually is requires strong, steadfast faith and a daily commitment to choose the right path. Yielding to the power of His grace and the direction of the Holy Spirit is neither a comfortable nor an automatic process!

"When looking back on the lives of men and women of God the tendency is to say: What wonderfully astute wisdom they had! How perfectly they understood all God wanted!" declares Oswald Chambers in *My Utmost for His Highest*. But, he continues, "the astute mind behind is the Mind of God, not human wisdom at all.

"We give credit to human wisdom when we should give credit to the Divine guidance of God through childlike people who were foolish enough to trust God's wisdom and the supernatural equipment of God."

Sounds like Mary of Bethany, doesn't it? She was foolish enough to trust God's wisdom.

"The man without the Spirit does not accept the things that come from the Spirit of God, for they are foolishness to him, and he cannot understand them, because they are spiritually discerned," proclaimed the apostle Paul (1 Cor. 2:14).

Although Mary's actions seemed utterly foolish, even wasteful, to the disciples at Simon's house that day, her sacrifice was highly praised and greatly valued by the Son of God. And His opinion is the one that counts!

❦ ❦ ❦ ❦ ❦

My Father, I abandon myself to You. Do with
me as You will.
Whatever You may do with me, I thank You.
I am prepared for anything, I accept everything,
provided Your will is fulfilled in me and in
all creatures—

I ask for nothing more, my God.
I place my soul in Your hands.
I give it to You, my God,
   with all the love of my heart,
   because I love You.
And for me it is a necessity of love,
   this gift of myself,
   this placing of myself in Your hands
   without reserve
     in boundless confidence
     because You are my Father.
             — CHARLES DE FOUCALD
             1858-1916

❦   ❦   ❦   ❦   ❦

Putting It Into Practice

"And the house was filled with
the fragrance of the perfume."

"Have I ever been carried away to do something for God not because it was my duty, nor because it was useful, nor because there was anything in it at all beyond the fact that I love Him?" asks Oswald Chambers.

"Have I ever realized that I can bring to God things that are of value to Him...not Divine, colossal things which could be recorded as marvelous, but ordinary, simple human things which will give evidence to God that I am abandoned to Him?

"Have I ever produced in the heart of the Lord what Mary of Bethany produced?"

Here it is! Through "ordinary, simple human things" we can express our womanhood as a fragrant offering to Jesus. Mary did it by washing Jesus' feet. In a spirit of love and worship, she seized the moment with what was at hand.

The simplest thing becomes a fragrant offering when it is given with love and humility for His glory. We don't have to wait for the perfect moment to surrender ourselves to God; the time to do it is right now, right where we are with what we have.

23

"There are times when it seems as if God watches to see if we will give Him the abandoned tokens of how genuinely we do love Him," Chambers continues. "Abandon to God is of more value than personal holiness."

"Personal holiness focuses on our own whiteness; we are greatly concerned about how we walk and talk and look, fearful lest we offend Him. Perfect love casts out all that when once we are abandoned to God. We have to get rid of this notion—'Am I of any use?'—and make up our minds that we are not, and we may be near the truth.

"It is never a question of being of use, but of being of value to God Himself. When we are abandoned to God, He works through us all the time."

❦   ❦   ❦   ❦   ❦

Lord, You said
that the most important commandment
was to love You
    with all of my heart,
    and all of my soul,
    and all of my mind,
    and all of my strength.
If You are to reign in my life,
if I proclaim You as LORD,
I will be set free to love You
more than anything or anyone else,
all day—
    from morning's awakening
    until evening's last thought.

All day
    a multitude of distractions
    compete with You
    for my attention.
Loving You first and foremost
is a Spirit-led decision.
I am thankful for the fire of my life
    burning deep within my soul,
    fueling my desire to be near You,

to worship at Your feet,
to totally depend upon Your strength.

May I give myself anew to You each day
as You fill me with Your love
and make my heart a nest
for Your descended Dove.

❧ ❧ ❧ ❧ ❧

Points to Ponder
—THEME: *Matthew 26:6-13*

When I think of Mary of Bethany's humility, I realize that the greatest obstacle to humility in my life is _____
_____
_____.

I feel I am "wasting my time" when I _____
_____
_____.

I do care what others think of me. I see this most often when _____
_____
_____.

"Abandonment to Christ" means _____
_____
_____
_____.

Additional Study
— MEDITATE ON Psalms 84, 86, 116.
— READ ABOUT an Old Testament woman, Abigail, in 1 Samuel 25.
— STUDY Philippians 2:1-11; Ephesians 5:1, 2, 8-21; and Matthew 16:24-26.
— MEMORIZE 1 John 2:17; Romans 12:1-3; and 1 Peter 5:6-7.

❧ ❧ ❧ ❧ ❧

Much-Afraid smiled and answered, "Why, yes, of course, I was forgetting," and she knelt down there in the wood, put a pile of stones together and laid sticks on them. As she noticed, altars are built of whatever materials lie close at hand at the time.

Then she hesitated. What should she lay on the altar this time?

She looked at the tiny swelling on the plant of love which might be a bud and again might not, then she leaned forward, placed her heart on the altar and said, "Behold me, here I am; thy little handmaiden Acceptance-with-Joy and all that is within my heart is thine."

—HANNAH HURNARD

Choosing

*"Martha, Martha," the Lord answered,
"you are worried and upset about many
things, but only one thing is needed.
Mary has chosen what is better, and it
will not be taken away from her."*
—LUKE 10:41-42

Choose—day after day. Choose to sit in
the dark and wait for His guidance.
Choose to sit at His feet and accept the
completeness of His truth. Choose as
Mary did in Luke 10, as she sat at Jesus'
feet and concentrated on what He was
teaching. It was not that Jesus was saying that housework was unnecessary—
He Himself cooked fish for the disciples
—but that there was at that time a choice
to be made.... Day by day and moment by
moment, choose carefully whom you will
listen to and whom you will serve.

— EDITH SCHAEFFER

The knowledge of God is very far from the
love of Him.

— BLAISE PASCAL
1623-1662

28

*I*t's another Monday morning. The clock radio goes off, and the six o'clock news vies with the warmth and pleasantness of your cozy nest of blankets. Another day lies before you. Time to face all the things that kept you awake last night. Just another day.

Another *new* day, unlike any other. A fresh slate, without marks. The birds outside the window seem to be aware of this as they greet the sunrise with song. "Praise You, heavenly Father, all honor and glory to Your holy name!" might be a comparable human refrain. But rather than greet the new day with this line of thanksgiving, we are more likely to...groan...yawn...and stumble to meet it sleepy-eyed.

The familiar story of Mary and Martha contains a valuable lesson for those of us who tend to feel weighed down by the pressures of life rather than lifted up by the realization that God is with us. Unlike the robins and sparrows, our level of thanksgiving is determined by choice rather than instinct. Only we humans can decide what to set our minds upon!

In the seventeenth century Francis Quarles wrote, "In having all things but Thee, what have I? Not having Thee, what have my labors got? Let me enjoy but Thee, what further crave I? And having Thee alone, what have I not?"

Indeed, if we belong to Jesus and if His Spirit has found a home within our hearts, what do we lack? Yet it is easy to forget this central truth when our lives get piled high with activity or when we are stressed out and exhausted from daily demands.

Becoming a fragrant offering is truly a day by day, even a moment by moment, decision.

❦   ❦   ❦   ❦   ❦

"Lord, don't You care that
my sister has left me to do
the work by myself? Tell her
to help me!"

Hassled and harried, it seemed

the right question to ask:
"Lord, don't You care?"

Think about it—
Wouldn't you have asked
the same thing?

When there is work to be done,
and few who will labor,
our patience wears thin.
We can get so busy serving Jesus
that we forget to give our Guest
the attention He deserves.
Taking time out
to be with the Lord
even seems like a waste of time.
Like Martha, we find the words
rising up inside, right next
to our frustration, and then:
"Lord, don't You care?"

Two thousand years later,
would His answer be
exactly the same?

❧ ❧ ❧ ❧ ❧

Considering the Challenge
"Lord, don't You care?"

Have you ever found yourself wondering whether God cares? Have you, like Martha, been challenged by someone else's devotion to Christ, only to discover yourself resenting that person?

Our natural inclination when we're under pressure is to compare, to blame, and to criticize others. Martha, no doubt, was sincerely going about her business when she finally reached her stress limit. But Jesus did not offer her His sympathy. Instead, He offered a gentle rebuke.

"The spiritual man is concerned with things of the spirit," writes Paul to the Romans. Living in accordance with the Holy Spirit transforms our outlook entirely. The more we yield ourselves to His direction, the less we find ourselves worrying about the things that do not matter to the Lord.

Anne Ortlund expresses it this way: "We must know intellectually and experientially that God is first. He must be our lives—in a class all by himself. Everything in our lives must converge at that one point: Christ."

Choosing to wait upon the Lord and let go of our anxiety about the cares of each day means recognizing the one thing Jesus said is needed: to "seek first his kingdom and his righteousness" (Matt. 6:33). Taking time out to be with Jesus—whether it means going to a quiet place to be alone, or praying while we do the dishes or while we drive to the store or while we shuttle the school car pool—can provide us with hidden strength that can never be taken away from us.

❦ ❦ ❦ ❦ ❦

Open, Lord, my inward ear,
And bid my heart rejoice!
Bid my quiet spirit hear
Thy comfortable voice.
Never in the whirlwind found,
Or where earthquakes rock the place;
Still and silent is the sound,
The whisper of Thy grace.

From the world of sin, and noise,
And hurry, I withdraw;
For the small and inward voice
I wait, with humble awe.
Silent am I now, and still,
Dare not in Thy presence move;
To my waiting soul reveal
The secret of Thy love.

Lord, my time is in Thine hand,
My soul to Thee convert;
Thou canst make me understand,
Though I am slow of heart;

Thine, in whom I love and move,
Thine the work, the praise is Thine,
Thou art wisdom, power and love—
And all Thou art is mine.
— CHARLES WESLEY
1707-1788

Putting It Into Practice
"Mary has chosen what is better."

In *The Practice of the Presence of God* we are introduced to a monk named Brother Lawrence, a man who found great joy in thinking about Jesus. "We should establish ourselves in God so that we sense His presence," he said. "The way to do that is [by] having lots of conversations with God...it is downright shameful to cut off a conversation with God to think about trifles or fooleries. More, we should feed and nourish our souls with high and noble thoughts about God. Those high thoughts give us great joy, and increase our devotion to God."

Like Mary, who chose the better way by taking time to sit at Jesus' feet and listen to Him, we need to practice being in His presence.

Brother Lawrence believed that we can "be absolutely faithful in dry times, insensitive times, and downright annoying times." For him, becoming a living sacrifice, a fragrant offering, made even mundane duties delightful experiences, unlike Martha who was so harried by the immediate that she took her eyes off the eternal.

"Really, we must give ourselves completely to God, both physically and spiritually," said Brother Lawrence, "seeking fulfillment in doing His will. His will may lead us through some pretty rough experiences or through some pretty nice experiences. Whichever, the truly surrendered person will have peace and inward knowledge that God is with him."

Mary's behavior was unconventional (it would have been unusual for a woman of that day to sit with men and listen to the teaching of a rabbi), while Martha busied herself with the things normally allotted to women. Yet Jesus commended

Mary and gently rebuked Martha for being more worried about her daily cares than she was about taking time with Him.

❦　❦　❦　❦　❦

Lord, Your love for me is
    beautiful,
        remarkable,
            and eternal.

Believing that You love me
    so completely
requires me to let go
    of the things that pull me
        away from You.

Like Martha,
    I tend to stumble
        under the weight of my needs
until I learn to trust You.

Only when I take my eyes
    off my self and look
        to You
do I begin to see the Big Picture.

I am thankful
    for Your presence here,
for becoming my guest
    in such finite dwellings.

I have chosen to open my door
    to You, Lord.
Enter my heart and abide
    with me
        always!

Teach me to stop and listen
    when I get too busy
        to hear Your voice
and accept Your word with joy.

Tame the Martha in me
    as I learn to sit with Mary
        on the floor
           at Your feet.

May I praise Your name
    each morning
        as I rise to greet the dawn,
giving You thanks
    for visiting with me
        as I walk through the day
           You have planned.

My times, dear Jesus,
    are in Your hands.

❦   ❦   ❦   ❦   ❦

Points to Ponder
    —*THEME: Luke 10:38-42*

When I woke up this morning, my first thought was _____
_____.

I have a tendency to worry about _____
_____.

The amount of time I spend worrying compared to the time
I spend listening to Jesus through prayer and Bible study is
_____.

When Jesus told Martha, "Mary has chosen what is better,"
He meant _____
_____.

Additional Study

    — *MEDITATE ON* Psalms 19, 23, and 27.
    — *READ ABOUT* an Old Testament woman, Ruth,
      in Ruth 1:1-18.

— *STUDY* Colossians 3:1-4; Philippians 4:4-8; and
Matthew 6:25-34.
— *MEMORIZE* John 14:27; 1 Samuel 22:31-33; and
Psalm 145:17-18.

❦ ❦ ❦ ❦ ❦

*You may rest assured of this, that all the
resources of God's infinite grace will be
brought to bear on the growing of the tiniest
flower in His spiritual garden, as certainly
as they are in His earthly creation; and as
the violet abides peacefully in its little place,
content to receive its daily portion without
concerning itself about the wandering of the
winds, or the falling of the rain, so must we
repose in the present moment as it comes to
us from God, contented with our daily portion, and without anxious thought about
anything that might be whirling around us
in God's glorious universe, sure that all
things will be made to "prosper" for us.*

— HANNAH WHITALL SMITH
1832-1911

Turning

Jesus said to her, "Mary!"
She turned toward him and cried out...,
"Rabboni!"
—JOHN 20:16

*To be in, but not of means to be delivered
from the spirit of this age and walk in
liberty as sons and daughters of God.*
>—JOHN WHITE

*How will you find good?
It is not a thing of choices;
it is a river that flows
from the foot of the invisible throne, and
flows by the path of obedience.*
>—GEORGE ELIOT
>(MARY ANN EVANS)
>*1819-1880*

*If you lean more on your own brain,
on your own work, than on the conquering
power of Christ, rarely and slowly will the
light illumine you.*
>—THOMAS A KEMPIS
>*1380-1471*

"I have seen the Lord!"

Mary Magdalene carried this exciting message back to the disciples after her encounter with Jesus at the tomb, for she was the first to see Him after His resurrection. What a privilege! But that privilege required something of Mary, and that was her persistent, single-minded attempt to locate the body of her Lord, as well as her willingness to turn away from the tomb when she heard His voice. Only then did she recognize her Master.

Commitment to Christ requires single-mindedness. However, this kind of devotion takes a supernatural strength that can only be produced by the Holy Spirit working in our lives. As the Spirit leads us into a deeper awareness of Christ's Lordship, our thoughts and feelings are brought more completely under His authority. Then the Spirit's fruit—love, joy, peace, patience, kindness, goodness, faithfulness, gentleness, and self-control—can be produced within us and experienced in abundance.

"Some of us are trying to offer up spiritual sacrifices to God before we have sacrificed the natural," warns Oswald Chambers. *"Sanctification means more than deliverance from sin; it means the deliberate commitment of myself whom God has saved to God, and I do not care what it costs.* If we do not sacrifice the natural to the spiritual, the natural life will mock at the Son of God in us and produce a continual swither."

I can identify with that word "swither." Can you? When my commitment wavers, when my love for Him is neither wholehearted nor single-minded, then I find myself "swithering" back and forth between the life I know Christ wants me to live and the worldly life I am drawn to when my eyes are off Him.

But living in the world does not mean we are doomed to be of it! Day by day, we can choose. Moment by moment, we can ask the Lord to lead us, strengthen us, and sustain us through His Spirit. Then our single-mindedness becomes a source of holy protection. As our hearts are drawn toward the kingdom of God and our minds are set on the things of

God, we are protected from the wiles of Satan.

"Jesus Christ lives indeed in the presence of the Father," states Francis Schaeffer in *True Spirituality*. "This is where we are called to live. We are to be dead in this present life."

When Mary turned away from death and the tomb, she recognized her Lord and knew He was alive.

❧   ❧   ❧   ❧   ❧

Break forth, O my soul!
  Sing for joy!
From death into life,
From darkness to light,
  Arise!
Dance on this day,
  This glorious day!
Turn away from His tomb,
The Savior has come,
  He's alive!
He's calling my name,
He shattered the grave,
  I'm alive!
Exalt Him on high!
  Lift up the great King!
  Let all heaven sing!

❧   ❧   ❧   ❧   ❧

Considering the Challenge
"She turned around...
but she did not realize that it was Jesus."

Have you ever had to turn all the way around before you could recognize the presence of the Lord and rejoice in it? Has some habit or something from your past obscured your view?

Even though she heard His voice, Mary had to turn away from the tomb and toward Jesus before she recognized Him, and the same is true for us. Memories and feelings from the past pull us back toward thoughts and behavior patterns associated with our "tombs"; a song, a photograph, even a specific scent can quickly revive remembrance of a dead relationship or the pain of an almost-forgotten wound.

But we need not fear the "skeletons" in our closets. Like Mary of Magdala, we can turn our backs to the grave as we learn to distinguish Jesus' call from other voices competing for our attention. Day by day we can choose to turn toward the reality of our new life in Christ, and in so doing we will see the Lord more clearly and recognize His voice.

"We are to be dead—not unconscious, not locked away in some darkness, but alive to God in communion with him, in communication with him," states Francis Schaeffer. "Our call to faith in this present life is that we should live as though dead to *all* things, that we might be alive to God...to love God enough to be contented; to love him enough in this present world to say, 'Thank you' in all the ebb and flow of life."

"Just as Christ was raised from the dead through the glory of the Father, we too may live a new life," Paul announced to the Romans. "If we have been united with him like this in his death, we will certainly also be united with him in his resurrection. For we know that our old self was crucified with him so that the body of sin might be done away with, that we should no longer be slaves to sin—because anyone who has died has been freed from sin. Now if we died with Christ, we believe that we will also live with him" (Rom. 6:4-8).

Dead...buried...and back to life again! Dead to sin but alive to God. The empty tomb is indeed behind us; *Jesus is calling our names!*

Turning away from our past way of life, from all that would hinder us from recognizing our *new* life in Christ, enables us to walk forth with Him in liberty. And as we experience the continual companionship of our risen Savior, we can rejoice and proclaim: "I have seen the Lord!"

❦   ❦   ❦   ❦   ❦

O God, thou art my God, I seek thee early
    with a heart that thirsts for thee
    and a body wasted with longing for thee,

like a dry and thirsty land that has no water.
So longing, I come before thee in the sanctuary
　　to look upon thy power and glory.
Thy true love is better than life;
　　therefore I will sing thy praises.
And so I bless thee all my life
　　and in thy name lift up my hands in prayer.
I am satisfied as with a rich feast
　　and wake the echoes with thy praise.
When I call thee to mind upon my bed
　　and think on thee in the watches of the night,
remembering how thou hast been my help
　　and that I am safe in the shadow of thy wings,
then I humbly follow thee with all my heart,
　　and thy right hand is my support.
　　　　　　　—PSALM 63:1-8 NEB

❧　❧　❧　❧　❧

Putting It Into Practice
"Why are you weeping?"

"What most of us need above everything else is to get away from ourselves, to forget ourselves," asserts Martyn Lloyd-Jones in *The Cross*.

"But we revolve around ourselves. We are the centre of our universe and we are always looking at ourselves, and everything is judged and evaluated in terms of us—what it means to me, what it does to me. All our rivalries, all our bitterness and jealousies come out of that. It is true of individuals, it is true of nations. Self-centredness.

"And then in addition to that, selfishness of course. Wanting everything for this self. No wonder Paul says we should no longer live unto ourselves but unto him who died for us and rose again."

Mary of Magdala had witnessed the Crucifixion; she had seen Joseph of Arimathea place Jesus' body in the tomb. Despite this and others' opinions about the Lord's death, Mary kept her vigil at the tomb. Even in His death, she wanted to be near the One who had given her new life.

Mary wasn't thinking of herself that Easter morning. She was willing to take risks, including the disapproval of others. Her love for her Lord had become the controlling factor in her life, and with the events of Good Friday indelibly printed on her soul, her life would never be the same again. The cross of Christ, and her identification with it, had separated Mary from the world and made her part of the kingdom of God.

"Once a man sees the message of the cross," Dr. Lloyd-Jones continues, "he has an entirely new view of everything. He is not just trying to live a good life now; not just trying to do no harm; not trying to live just on the edge of the law—not wanting to be prosecuted, but going as far as he safely can.

"That is all finished. He is a new man. He has been bought with a price; he is a son of God. He is being prepared for him. He has a new motive. *To sin now means that he is wounding love....* He is wounding the love of the one who gave himself for him.

"He says, I cannot do it. I have been bought with a price. I have no right to do it. I am not my own. I belong to him. I am a slave of Christ as I used to be a slave of the devil and of sin. I have no right to, and I cannot do it.

"He has a new conception of sin, he has new motives for living a holy life, and thank God, over and above all, he has got a new power whereby to do it."

❦　❦　❦　❦　❦

Lord, I know from experience
that You came to set women free,
    not just temporarily,
        but for all eternity.
Your kind of freedom requires faith
    instead of legislation; hope
        instead of a vote.
It has nothing to do with self-sufficiency.
        Choices, made moment to moment;
        decisions, taken step by step;
            learning about liberation
            from Your point of view.

43

I am thankful for the price You paid
    to open the pathway
        out of captivity
           once and for all.
Through Your broken body,
    You have asked me to enter
        the kingdom of heaven.
I am no longer bound
    to this world!
With shouts of joy,
    I proclaim Your victory
        and walk forth together
           with those You have called by name.

Jesus, show me how to love You wholeheartedly,
    to be single-minded in my obedience to
        Your Word!
I ask You to revive me daily with the power
    of the Holy Spirit.
Send Your living waters, Lord!
    Breathe upon me,
    work within me,
        that I might come *fully alive*
          in You,
           my Redeemer and Savior,
    for Your honor and glory.

❧   ❧   ❧   ❧   ❧

Points to Ponder
    —THEME: *John 20:10-17*

At this time in my life the most difficult area to surrender to
Christ's Lordship is _____
_____
_____.

Since becoming a believer, my attitude toward the world and
my behavior within it has _____
_____
_____.

The most difficult part of turning away from my past is
_____
_____.

Loving the Lord wholeheartedly means _____
_____
_____.

I know that I cannot love the Lord perfectly, but I can
_____
_____.

Additional Study

— *MEDITATE ON* Psalms 4, 20, and 30.
— *READ ABOUT* an Old Testament woman, Jehosheba, in2 Chronicles 22:10-12.
— *STUDY* Ephesians 2:1-10; Romans 8:1-17; and John 14:15-26.
— *MEMORIZE* Colossians 2:6-7; Isaiah 60:1; and Psalm 56:12-13.

❧ ❧ ❧ ❧ ❧

Everything that is a mere form, a mere habit and custom in divine things, is to be dreaded exceedingly: life, power, reality, this is what we have to aim after. Things should not result from without, but from within. The sort of clothes I wear, the kind of house I live in, the quality of the furniture I use, all such things should not result from other persons doing so and so, or because it is customary among those brethren with whom I associate to live in a simple, inexpensive, self-denying way. Whatever be done in these things, in the way of giving up, or self-denial, or dead-ness to the world, should result from the joy we have in God, and from the entering into the preciousness of our future inheritance...- we should begin the thing in a right way, that is, aim after the right state of heart;

begin inwardly instead of outwardly. If otherwise, it will not last. We shall look back, or even get into a worse state than we were before.

But oh! how different if joy in God leads us to any little act of self-denial. How gladly we do it then! How great an honour then do we count it to be! How much does the heart then long to be able to do more for Him who has done so much for us!

—GEORGE MÜLLER

1805-1898

Walking

When they heard what he said, one by one they went away, the eldest first; and Jesus was left alone, with the woman still standing there.

—JOHN 8:9 NEB

God creates out of nothing.
Wonderful, you say.
Yes, to be sure,
but He does what is still more wonderful:
He makes saints out of sinners.
—SOREN KIERKEGAARD
1813-1855

The Christian walk is much like riding a
bicycle; we are either moving forward or
falling off.
—ROBERT TUTTLE

"If any one of you is without sin,
let him be the first to throw a stone at her."

T his was Jesus' response to the Pharisees who would have stoned the woman caught in adultery. To the woman herself, Jesus said, "I do not condemn you. Go and leave your life of sin." A short time later He said to the people gathered around Him, perhaps in her hearing, "I am the light of the world. Whoever follows me will never walk in darkness, but will have the light of life" (John 8:12).

The Scripture tells us very little about this woman who was brought to Jesus. Possibly she had been trapped for some time by the dark mesh of sexual sin. "Sins are like mushrooms," explains Dick Keyes in *Beyond Identity*. "They grow best in the dark." But in Jesus' words were the implicit promise that she did not have to stay in darkness; her life could be different.

When I read this brief passage, I think of women today who are trapped in the darkness and confusion of sin. Not in a spirit of condemnation, for we are all sinners saved by grace. Rather, my heart aches for them. So much of what passes for glamour in our world (even the life of a prostitute like the Mayflower Madam), set forth as enviable in life-styles portrayed on film, on television, or in gossip-hungry magazines, degrades the meaning of womanhood. Yet women today are prompted to emulate it.

How much we need to hear and heed Jesus' promise that He will light our way with His love and grace and protective Spirit. By actively walking with Christ, we are empowerd to conform to His will; and as we walk, we build ourselves up in faith. Then, when we find ourselves struggling with sin, we know it is because we have yet to expose it to His light.

Blaise Pascal described this eloquently when he wrote, "It is true there is difficulty entering into godliness. But this difficulty does not arise from the religion which begins in us, but only from the irreligion which is still there. If our senses were not opposed to penitence, if our corruption were not opposed to the purity of God, there would be nothing in this painful to us." Following Jesus, in other words, is contrary to our lower nature. Walking in the light is painful to our naked eyes!

So what can we do? We aren't told what the woman did. Her response depended, as does ours, on whether she was willing to yield to the supernatural grace of God, who leads onward and upward into holiness. He offers us, as He did her, a way out of the darkness through confession and repentance, but it's up to us; we must decide whether to follow where He leads. What an offer!

Why be satisfied with the dank, moldy scent of mushrooms when we can enjoy the sun-drenched fragrance of the Rose of Sharon?

No matter what we have done or how unclean we may feel inside, Jesus is waiting for us to walk with Him. He will not condone what we have done, but He will not condemn us. Instead, He admonishes us to leave our life of sin and walk with Him into the light of eternity.

❦   ❦   ❦   ❦   ❦

The older ones left first....

I think I understand now,
   as I picture them leaving
      one
         by
            one.
Jesus' words cut deep,
   dividing *soul* and *spirit,*
      separating *joint* and *marrow,*
         judging the *thoughts* and *attitudes*
         of the heart.

  Nothing in all creation is hidden
    from God's sight.
The Word of God is living and active still;
   I tremble in awe before Him.

❦   ❦   ❦   ❦   ❦

Considering the Challenge
"Then neither do I condemn you," Jesus declared.

I wonder what thoughts raced through the woman's mind as the Pharisees dragged her before Jesus. Was she hardened to a life of sin and thus resigned to such treatment? I don't think so. Her response is not the response of a hardened woman. Or perhaps she was merely responding to the love and acceptance in Jesus' words.

Have you ever approached the Lord expecting Him to punish and condemn you, only to be overcome by His mercy and grace? Has He ever ministered His love and healing to you just when you felt you deserved His rejection? How easy and natural it is to believe the Lord is a Pharisee who would stone us to death as our sin deserves!

"Each time you fall," says C.S. Lewis in *Mere Christianity,* "He will pick you up again. And He knows perfectly well that your own efforts are never going to bring you anywhere near perfection." Thus, we should not be discouraged by the Lord's demand for perfection; for even when we fail in our attempts to be good, the Lord is faithful in His promises to us.

But make no mistake about it: the work of the Holy Spirit is to guide us toward that perfection, toward holiness. There are no loopholes in the Christian life, no detours on the walk of faith.

"No power in the universe, except yourself, can prevent the Lord from taking us to that goal," Lewis explains. "We may be content to remain what we call 'ordinary people': but he is determined to carry out quite a different plan. To shrink back from that plan is not humility; it is laziness and cowardice. To submit to it is not conceit...it is obedience."

The secret of this amazing, glorious, strenuous climb is Christ in us, the hope of glory!

Jesus loves us so much that He will accomplish our *complete restoration* through the process we call *sanctification.* He isn't just out to make us whole; He's out to make us holy. Although we must wait until we meet Him to receive the fullness of all that this means, our obedience to

His Word, by the power of the Holy Spirit working in our lives, will bring us ever closer to this goal.

As we learn to submit to God's unflagging efforts to change us from the inside out, our true identity will slowly but surely be conformed to the image of His Son.

❧ ❧ ❧ ❧ ❧

Lord, we come before Thee now,
At Thy feet we humbly bow;
O do not our suit disdain!
Shall we seek Thee, Lord, in vain?

Lord, on Thee our souls depend;
In compassion now descend,
Fill our hearts with Thy rich grace,
Tune our lips to sing Thy praise.

Send some message from Thy word
That may joy and peace afford;
Let Thy Spirit now impart
Full salvation to each heart.

Comfort those who weep and mourn,
Let the time of joy return;
Those that are cast down lift up,
Make them strong in faith and hope.

Grant that all may seek and find
Thee a God supremely kind;
Heal the sick, the captive free;
Let us all rejoice in Thee.

—WILLIAM HAMMOND
1719-1783

❧ ❧ ❧ ❧ ❧

Putting It Into Practice
"Go now and leave your life of sin."

Walking is wonderful exercise, but to get results we must do it faithfully—and that requires discipline. Maybe on the first days of spring we are anxious to get out in the warm sunshine and fresh breeze. Or perhaps October's "bright blue weather" lures us outdoors to amble through colorful fallen leaves. But most of the time walking requires determination, discipline, and effort. Like everything else that's good for us, it does not come naturally or easily.

Why are so many Christians today content to be what C.S. Lewis called "ordinary people"? Why do we just want to be superficially changed when we can be totally restored to wholeness? Is it because it's too risky? Or too difficult?

"We are so involved in the products of life—finding a mate, getting a degree, acquiring a job—that we fail to take time to observe the process God is using to get us to the product," states Christian counselor Earl Wilson in *The Undivided Self*. "If you are a tennis buff and a friend invites you to watch the Wimbledon finals, you would not be satisfied only to look at the scoreboard at the end of the first set. You would want to know how it happened. If you did watch the whole match, you would marvel at the skill and strategy that went into the winning effort. Likewise we should take time to observe God's action in our lives. When we do savor him we say, 'God is trustworthy and he is enabling me.' God must not be taken for granted. Savor the Savior! A delightful way to live."

Dr. Wilson goes on to say that as we are able to trust God's work in our lives, we find that He asks us to trust Him in more difficult areas and in new ways.

"Learning to trust God in the more difficult areas," says Wilson, "comes when we are willing to risk growing. Only if we want to grow will we grow.... Too often in life we trust God for solutions to problems, but we only want the quick and easy solution."

Likening spiritual restoration to home remodeling, Wilson makes a vivid point about the Christian walk: "Usually we want God to redecorate us. The quickest and least costly method is the preferred one. However, the conflict comes when God, the Master Builder, recognizes that our needs are really for remodeling, not just paint and wallpaper. We may resist him and ask, 'Why? Why can't you do it my way? Why do I have to go through all this pain? Why would you allow me to go through this if you really love me?"... Taking gradually bigger steps of faith and having a more consistent willingness to walk while trusting God are the common touchstones of growth in Christ."

❦ ❦ ❦ ❦ ❦

Lord, help me to understand
   the difference between
      conviction and condemnation,
to never forget that it is always
   Your *loving-kindness*
      that is leading me
         to restoration and victory.
Surround me with compassionate tenacity
   as You tend the boundary lines
      of my daily walk;
keep me from straying
   beyond hearing distance.
Gentle shepherd,
   tune my ears
      to the timbre of Your voice.

I do not care to listen
   to the confusing chorus
      of Your enemies.

I am thankful
for the way
You have chosen to care
for Your flock—
following Your direction
and heeding Your call
brings me joy as well as
protection, life
instead of destruction.

Dear Lord, help me to come running
   whenever You call,

to follow
   wherever You lead,
to do
  whatever You ask.
It is in Your name, Jesus,
that I pray these things.

❦   ❦   ❦   ❦   ❦

Points to Ponder
   —THEME: John 8:2-11

I am greatly encouraged by Jesus' response to the woman in John 8 because _____
_____.

When I lack self-control or know I have sinned, confession and repentance _____
_____.

Knowing that the Lord loves me enough to bring about my complete restoration makes me realize that _____
_____
_____.

Rather than being discouraged by my failures, I _____
_____
_____.

It is difficult for me to accept God's forgiveness when _____
_____
_____.

Additional Study

   —MEDITATE ON Psalms 51, 32, 130, and 119:9-48.
   — READ ABOUT an Old Testament woman, Rahab, in Joshua 2, 6:22-25.
   — STUDY Hebrews 10:19-23; 1 Peter 1:13—2:3; 1 John 1:5—2:2; and Isaiah 61.
   — MEMORIZE Romans 8:1-2 and Proverbs 28:13.

❦   ❦   ❦   ❦   ❦

There are no shortcuts to holiness. There is no easy way to conquer the flesh. Christian character is a matter of growth, not of secrets or formulas. Growth takes time. It also takes the discipline of prayer, of study, of heart searching, of sensitivity to the Holy Ghost's pleading, and of consistent obedience. We live in an age of instant coffee and fast food joints. But there is no instant solution for carnality. It must always begin with a renewed awareness of our sin, a daily renewed thankfulness for the never-ending grace of God, and a sense of being set free repeatedly to a life of holiness.

—JOHN WHITE

PART TWO

Reflections on Abiding in Christ

*For the grace of God has dawned upon
the world with healing for all mankind;
and by it we are disciplined to renounce
godless ways and worldly desires,
and to live a life of temperance, honesty,
and godliness in the present age,
looking forward to the happy fulfillment
of our hope when the splendor of
our great God and Savior
Jesus Christ will appear.*
—TITUS 2:11-13 NEB

Love divine, all loves excelling,
Joy of heaven to earth come down,
Fix in us Thy humble dwelling,
All Thy faithful mercies crown.
Jesus, Thou art all compassion,
Pure, unbounded love Thou art;
Visit us with Thy salvation,
Enter every trembling heart.

Breathe, O breathe Thy loving Spirit
Into every troubled breast;
Let us all in Thee inherit,
Let us find Thy promised rest.
Take away our bent to sinning,
Alpha and Omega be;
End of faith, as its beginning,
Set our hearts at liberty.

Come, Almighty to deliver,
Let us all Thy life receive;
Suddenly return, and never,
Nevermore Thy temples leave.
Thee we would be always blessing,
Serve Thee as Thy hosts above,
Pray, and praise Thee without ceasing,
Glory in Thy perfect love.

Finish then Thy new creation,
Pure and spotless let us be;
Let us see Thy great salvation
Perfectly restored in Thee.
Changed from glory into glory,
'Til in heaven we take our place,
'Til we cast our crowns before Thee,
Lost in wonder, love, and praise.
— CHARLES WESLEY
1707-1788

Abiding

*She [Anna] never left the temple
but worshiped night and day,
fasting and praying.*
—LUKE 2:27

I seek at the beginning to get my heart
into such a state that it has no will of its
own in a given matter. Nine-tenths of the
trouble with people is generally just there.
Nine-tenths of the difficulties are over-
come when our hearts are ready to do the
Lord's will, whatever it may be. When
one truly is in this state, it is usually but
a little way to the knowledge of what His
will is.
—GEORGE MÜLLER
1805-1898

Spread out your petition before God, and
then say, "Thy will, not mine, be done."
The sweetest lesson I have learned in God's
school is to let the Lord choose for me.
—DWIGHT L. MOODY
1837-1899

In His will is our peace.
—DANTE ALLIGHERI
1265-1321

*"*bide in me, and I in you.... If ye keep my commandments, ye shall abide in my love," Jesus said to His disciples shortly before His death as He prepared them to live the Christian life (John 15:4, 10 KJV).

"These words are no law of Moses, demanding from the sinful what they cannot perform," declares Andrew Murray. "They are the command of love." They are the words of the Bridegroom seeking to protect His beloved; the words of the Shepherd diligently guarding His flock; the words of the Teacher faithfully instructing His disciples.

Jesus invites us to enter into His life and *abide:* to remain in His presence on good days and bad, whether we feel worthy of His love or not. Abiding is a constant state, no matter what life brings with the new day—a splitting headache, a disrupted schedule, a phone that never quits.

Abiding in Christ...keeping His commandments. This is the deeply rooted foundation upon which believers build. Then, firmly planted, we are able to stand against the strongest winds of winter and in season to bear fruit for the kingdom of God. Good works, spiritual gifts, holiness—all the things we associate with what it means to be a disciple—come out of abiding. They blossom from the nourishment we receive from total dependence upon Jesus and His Word.

"Abiding in Him," explains Andrew Murray, "is not a work that we have to do as the condition for enjoying His salvation, but a consenting to let Him do all for us, and in us, and through us. It is a work He does for us—the fruit and the power of His redeeming love. Our part is simply to yield, to trust, and to wait for what He has engaged to perform."

Yielding. Trusting. Waiting. Certainly those words apply to Anna, the woman we meet in Luke 2:36-38. We know little else about her, but we know she was willing to abide and wait, for Luke says she worshiped in the Temple day and night, fasting and praying. She abided in worship and obedience, waiting for the Messiah.

To many this might sound like a wasted life—or perhaps even an easy one. Yet apparently Anna had known her share of sorrow. She had been married only seven years when her husband died, and she lived as a widow until she was eighty-four. Sad? Lonely? We don't know. But whatever her circumstances, she devoted her life to the Lord and He led her into holiness. The Scriptures call her a prophetess.

And God rewarded her faithfulness in a special way, for she was present when Joseph and Mary brought baby Jesus to the Temple. She thanked God for Him and spoke to all who were there about the Messiah who would redeem Israel.

Anna made a choice. It couldn't always have been easy, but day by day, she chose to abide with God—as we must. And as we make that choice, we too will be rewarded.

When we call upon the Lord, realizing our complete dependence upon Him, we are drawn deeper into an intimate relationship with Him. Then we yield, we trust, we wait, acutely aware of our need for God and our need to abide in His Word.

Surely Anna's life was one of the most fragrant offerings ever brought to the Temple. Ours can be too!

❧ ❧ ❧ ❧ ❧

She never left the Temple,
but stayed there night and day—
worshiping,
fasting,
praying...
waiting.
Dwelling with You, Lord,
for years and years and years—
and still not too old
or too tired
to wait upon Your Word.

What was the secret
of her patience?
How could she wait
so long?

I wish I could have been there
when she met You face to face!
I know she would have told me
much about You.

❦   ❦   ❦   ❦   ❦

Considering the Challenge
"She gave thanks to God."

"Holiness does not consist in mystic speculations, enthusiastic fervors, or uncommanded austerities; it consists in thinking as God thinks and willing as God wills," wrote nineteenth-century theologian John Brown.

Have you ever found yourself challenged by the Word of God to "think as God thinks and will as God wills"? Have you ever been surprised to discover that your obedience to God's Word produces "a harvest of righteousness" even when everything in your life seems to be working against you?

Because the Word of God is alive *within* us, it is possible for us to abide in Christ whatever the circumstances. Through yielding, trusting, waiting—abiding—in His Word we are continually nourished and upheld by the power of His life, as He promised.

To live and be healthy physically we need food; to abide and be healthy spiritually we need nourishment from God. This comes to us directly through His Word.

"The Word is that by which we live, namely, Jesus Himself; and His words represent, in part, in shadow, in suggestion, Himself. Any utterance worthy of being called *a truth*, is human food: how much more *the Word*, presenting no abstract laws of our being, but the vital relation of soul and body, heart and will, strength and rejoicing, beauty and light, to Him who first gave birth to them all!"

Thus George MacDonald, over a century ago, joyfully proclaimed the reality experienced by all who have made God's Word their home—their abiding place.

"Thanks be to God for his indescribable gift!" (2 Cor. 9:15).

❦   ❦   ❦   ❦   ❦

Be Thou my Vision, O Lord of my heart;
Nought be all else to me save that Thou art—

Thou my best thought, by day or by night,
Waking or sleeping, Thy presence my light.

Be Thou my Wisdom and Thou my true Word;
I ever with Thee and Thou with me, Lord;
Thou my great Father and I Thy true son;
Thou in me dwelling, and I with Thee one.

Riches I heed not, nor man's empty praise,
Thou mine inheritance, now and always:
Thou and Thou only, first in my heart,
High King of heaven, my Treasure Thou art.

High King of heaven, my victory won,
May I reach heaven's joys, O bright heaven's Sun!
Heart of my own heart, whatever befall,
Still be my Vision, O Ruler of all.
— ANCIENT IRISH HYMN
TRANS. BY MARY BYRNE

❦ ❦ ❦ ❦ ❦

Putting It Into Practice
"She...worshiped night and day, fasting and praying."

Anna's devotion to the Lord must have withstood many tests
and temptations—days when she just didn't feel like rising at
daybreak to petition the Lord in prayer, times when leaving
the Temple must have repeatedly crossed her mind. Yet
Anna remained faithful to God each day and, eventually, her
prayers were amply rewarded.

These verses in Luke describe a woman who spent most
of her lifetime dwelling in the shadow of the Lord's presence.
She spent decades being shaped and refined through devel-
oping intimacy with God.

For abiding isn't passive existing; it's painful growing.
Jesus said: "I am the real vine, and my Father is the gardener.
Every barren branch of mine he cuts away; and every fruiting
branch he cleans, to make it more fruitful still. You have
already been cleansed by the word I spoke to you. Dwell in

me, as I in you" (John 15:1-4 NEB).

Think for a moment about how grapevines grow. Is it by their own effort? Do they bear fruit only in perfect weather, or can a strong vine withstand certain fluctuations in its environment? Does the farmer tend and protect his vines to increase the yield?

"Do not trouble about your growing, but see to it that you have the growing life," wrote Hannah Whitall Smith. "Abide in the vine. Let the life from Him flow through all your spiritual veins. Put your growing into His hands as completely as you have put all your other affairs. Suffer Him to manage it as He will."

In a vineyard, pruning is necessary for the production of fruit. Without it, grapevines waste their energy maintaining portions of the plant that are barren. By cutting away or lopping off wandering, superficial plant growth, the vinedresser strengthens the vine's ability to direct its nutrients toward growing grapes instead of toward nourishing a worthless collection of twigs and leaves.

Pruning is like surgery. It is a rude shock to a grapevine. If plants could feel pain, an anesthetic would be required to make the process bearable.

Although pruning is traumatic and appears to nearly destroy the vine, something amazing takes place after the plant has been cut back. After a time of recuperation, the vine springs to life, eventually becoming more beautiful and productive than before. This principle is essential to vineyard life.

"Trust the Divine Husbandman absolutely, and always," continues Smith. "Accept each moment's dispensation as it comes to you from His dear hands as being needed sunshine or dew for the moment's growth." No matter what season of life you are in—whether you are being pruned, gathering strength, bearing fruit, or producing a harvest—you will be faithfully sustained by the Word of God as your heavenly Father manages your growth in grace.

"Discipline, no doubt, is never pleasant; at the time it seems painful, but in the end it yields for those who have been trained by it the peaceful harvest of an honest life" (Heb. 12:11 NEB).

Are you abiding in the vine? Are you dwelling within the Word of God? Then expect the Lord to prune you, nourish you, watch over you. Do not shrink back as He cuts away the barren parts of your life—the parts that cannot produce fruit or bring forth His righteousness.

God's vineyard is not always a comfortable place to abide, but take heart: yielding to the loving hand of the Gardener produces a bounty of eternal rewards.

❦   ❦   ❦   ❦   ❦

Lord, Your Word has taught me
    that to be fruitful,
        I must be faithful;
    to be peaceful,
        I must be hopeful;
    to be beautiful,
        I must be joyful.

Heavenly Father,
    I thank You
        for giving me the grace to grow
            through a *real* vine—
a vine that does not shrivel
    when the temperature rises,
a vine that will never be touched
    by disease or decay,
a vine that sends its life
    through every branch You clean.

Fill me with Your life, O Lord,
    as I place my faith
        in You alone—
    blossoming branches spilling forth
        the sweet fragrance of Your Son.
May I bear Your fruit,
    manifest Your peace
        and share Your beauty
in response to Your gifts
    of faith, hope and joy,
guarded forever
    by the patient nurture
        of Your steadfast love.

❦ ❦ ❦ ❦ ❦

Points to Ponder
—THEME: *Luke 2:22-38*

I am most aware of my need for God's Word when _____
_____
_____.

Yielding, trusting, and waiting are the most difficult for me
when _____
_____.

When I spend time reading the Word, I _____
_____
_____.

I know God is pruning me when _____
_____
_____.

Additional Study

- —*MEDITATE ON* Psalms 16, 25, and 91.
- —*READ ABOUT* an Old Testament woman, the Shunammite woman, in 2 Kings 4:8-37; 8:1-6.
- —*STUDY* Ephesians 3:16-20; Colossians 1:9-14; and Psalms 119:129-136, 169-176.
- —*MEMORIZE* Colossians 3:16; Isaiah 32:17; and Psalm 119:11.

❦ ❦ ❦ ❦ ❦

We have to form habits that express what God's grace has done in us. It is not a question of being saved from hell, but of being saved in order to manifest the life of the Son of God in our mortal flesh, and it is the disagreeable things which make us exhibit whether or not we are manifesting His life. Do I manifest the essential sweetness of the Son of God, or the essential irritation of "myself" apart from Him? The only thing that will enable me to enjoy the disagreeable is the keen enthusiasm of letting the life of the Son of God manifest itself in me. No matter how disagreeable a thing may be, say—"Lord, I am delighted to obey Thee in this matter," and instantly the Son of God will press to the front, and there will be manifested in my human life that which glorifies Jesus.

—OSWALD CHAMBERS

Seeking

A few men became followers of Paul and believed. Among them was...also a woman named Damaris....
— ACTS 17:33

In every heart He wishes to be first:
He therefore keeps the secret key Himself
To open all its chambers, and to bless
With perfect sympathy, and holy peace,
Each solitary soul which comes to Him.
—ANONYMOUS

The secret heart is devotion's temple; there
the saint lights the flame of purest
sacrifice, which burns unseen but not
unaccepted.
—HANNAH MORE
1745-1833

72

*T*he search for truth is age-old. Every century spawns new philosophies or religions, and in recent decades we have been inundated with a wide variety of techniques intended to expand human consciousness or restore the inner self. These are rooted in ancient mystical and occult practices and have simply been renamed or repackaged to appeal to modern minds.

Talk show hosts listen intently to each guest who offers a new or bizarre belief. Shirley MacLaine writes about reincarnation and other New Age theories, and her books make the best-seller list; a major network even airs a film based on her supposedly autobiographical tales. Magazines carry articles about the value of owning crystals, and the famous and not-so-famous become the proud possessors of rocks they hope will cure their ills or soothe their troubled souls. Seminars and classes on every new theory are readily available to any seeker.

First-century Athens, in the apostle Paul's day, had its share of philosophers and seekers, too. "All the Athenians and the foreigners who lived there *spent their time doing nothing but talking about and listening to the latest ideas*" (Acts 17:21). The city itself was filled with idols, including an altar "TO AN UNKNOWN GOD," a measure taken to guard against offending any god by overlooking him. They even had a council, the Areopagus, that spent its time dealing with any new religions or foreign gods. "They considered themselves the custodians of teachings that introduced new religions and foreign gods" (note on 17:19, *NIV Study Bible,* p. 1680).

Thus, when Paul began preaching the Good News about Jesus and His resurrection, he was taken before the Areopagus and questioned about this new teaching. "May we know what this new teaching is that you are presenting?" they said. "You are bringing some strange ideas to our ears, and we want to know what they mean" (vv. 19-20). But what did they hope to learn from Paul? Were they just following their usual practice of "doing nothing but talking about and listening to the latest ideas"?

"There is a seeking and finding which results in everlasting *life*. There is also a seeking and finding which ends in everlasting *death*. There is no neutral position," says Edith

Schaeffer, pointing out the critical difference between seeking to know Christ as Lord and seeking to understand Him for other reasons.

"There are individuals today who only seek Jesus in order to prove that He is not who He claims to be," she reminds us, as well as those "who spend a lifetime seeking to prove that Jesus is just a good man—not God, not the Second Person of the Trinity.... There are whole churches or groups within churches who use the words *seek* and *find* in relationship to Jesus, but who cast away His Word, who reduce the Bible to simple myths and fables with a variety of applications that change with the shifting winds.... It is a matter of life and death to the one seeking, whether the meaning of the search is for tearing apart, judging, criticizing, and destroying the Word of God, or whether the final meaning or intent of the search is to bow before the Living God and allow Him to do the 'finding' of that lost one. Jesus came to seek and to save the lost people, and so He clearly reveals Himself to the ones who are lost and truly want to be found."

Among those listening to Paul that day at the Areopagus was a woman named Damaris. As she listened to the apostle address the council and tell of "The God who made the world and everything in it...and does not live in temples built by hands" (v. 24), she found what she had been searching for.

❦   ❦   ❦   ❦   ❦

A few men became followers and believed...
also a woman named Damaris....

A *woman* at the Areopagus!
Damaris—
    what was it in your heart
       that came alive that day?
Did you feel Paul's words leap
    right to the center of your soul?
A new God he proclaimed to you,
    One who does not live in temples
       built by human hands.

The God who made the world and everything
in it, the Lord of heaven and earth!
In Him we live
and move
and have our being!
Who among the gods is like You, O Lord?
Who is like You—
majestic in holiness,
awesome in glory,
working wonders?
O Lord, what is man that You care for him?
O Lord, our Lord,
how majestic is Your name
in all the earth!
A Living God...
A Mighty God...
A Holy God....
Damaris—
I rejoice that you found
what you were searching for
that day!

❦ ❦ ❦ ❦ ❦

Considering the Challenge
"God did this
so men would seek him and...find him."

"How can we turn our knowledge *about* God into knowl-edge *of* God?" asks J. I. Packer in *Knowing God*. "The rule for doing this is demanding, but simple. It is that we turn each truth that we learn *about* God into a matter of medita-tion *before* God, leading to prayer and praise *to* God."

But isn't meditation something those Eastern religions practice, something to be avoided by Christians? How can it help us to know the King of Kings and Lord of Lords? Isn't just reading the Bible enough? "Meditation is the activity of calling to mind, and thinking over, and dwelling on, and applying to oneself, the various things that one knows about the works and ways and purposes and promises of God," explains Packer. "It is an activity of holy thought, consciously performed in the presence of God, under the eye of God, by the help of God, as a means of communion with God. Its purpose is to clear one's mental and spiritual vision of God, and to let His truth make its full and proper impact on one's mind and heart. It is a matter of talking to oneself about God and oneself; it is, indeed, often a matter of arguing with oneself, reasoning oneself out of moods of doubt and unbelief into a clear apprehension of God's power and grace. Its effect is ever to humble us, as we contemplate God's greatness and glory, and our own littleness and sinfulness, and to encourage and reassure us—'comfort' us, in the old, strong, Bible sense of the word—as we contemplate the unsearchable riches of divine mercy displayed in the Lord Jesus Christ."

To me, meditation implies not only moments of intense concentration, but also of quiet reflection; it means time spent searching for God while in the peaceful solitude of nature as well as time spent thinking about Him in the midst of everyday activities. Even a mundane job such as doing the dishes can be a delight when I am looking toward my heavenly King.

Before becoming a Christian, I took numerous yoga classes, practiced specific breathing techniques, and fine-tuned my dietary habits in search of spiritual bliss. While investing all this attention on my outward behavior, however, I was blind to the sin covering the inside of my heart. Meditating on meaningless images and phrases did absolutely nothing to improve my relationship with the one true God.

All of this changed when I met the Lord. I realized I had been seeking for truth in all the wrong places. But I found the Word of God confronted day-to-day reality as it actually is rather than merely giving me an escape hatch through which to flee the painful areas of my life.

"There is no virtue in minimizing the agony of suffering in a twisted world," writes Dick Keyes. "But the salvation of Jesus Christ is even greater and more wonderful than the Fall is horrible." Beyond the cross, the Good News of redemption promises eternal rewards for those who receive reconciliation through the blood of the Lamb.

Contemplating the "unsearchable riches of divine mercy" has provided me with an inexhaustible supply of wonder with which to fill my thought life. Seeking to dwell in the light of His presence has been a daily privilege—and challenge—that more than satisfies my hungry soul.

"May my meditation be pleasing to him, as I rejoice in the Lord," concluded the author of Psalm 104 (v. 34). May this be our attitude as we seek God in the daily reality of life and apply His Word within it. *Lord, help us to call to mind, think over, dwell on, and apply to our lives the things we know about You!*

❦ ❦ ❦ ❦ ❦

Jesus, Thou Joy of loving hearts,
Thou Fount of life, Thou Light of men,
From the best bliss that earth imparts,
We turn unfilled to Thee again.

Thy truth unchanged hath ever stood,
Thou savest those that on Thee call;
To them that seek Thee, Thou art good,
To them that find Thee, all in all.

We taste Thee, O Thou Living Bread,
And long to feast upon Thee still;
We drink of Thee, the Fountain-head,
And thirst our souls from Thee to fill.

Our restless spirits yearn for Thee,
Where'er our changeful lot is cast;
Glad when Thy gracious smile we see,
Blest when our faith can hold Thee fast.

O Jesus, ever with us stay,
Make all our moments calm and bright;
Chase the dark night of sin away,
Shed o'er the world Thy holy light.

— ATTR. TO BERNARD OF CLAIRVAUX
1091-1153

❦ ❦ ❦ ❦ ❦

Putting It Into Practice
"For in him we live and move and have our being."

Daily we are surrounded with the sights and sounds of a fast-paced world that competes with our need for spending time alone with God. Distractions arise everywhere, and whether out of necessity or our own desire, they keep us from Him. How often have you determined to set aside time for prayer or Bible reading, only to fail after a few attempts?

After spending more than ten years struggling to enter into a time of earnest, heartfelt prayer in the morning, George Müller discovered "that the first and primary business" he needed to attend to was to have his soul find happiness in the Lord. "I saw that the most important thing I had to do was give myself to the reading of the Word of God and to meditation on it...and that thus...my heart might be brought into experimental communion with the Lord."

He would begin by reflecting on the New Testament, "searching...into every verse to get blessing out of it...for the sake of obtaining food for my own soul." Reverend Müller found that this invariably "led to confession, or to thanksgiving, or to intercession, or supplication...turning all as I go into prayer for myself and others." Thus the Word led him into conversation with God.

"When we pray we speak to God. Now prayer, in order to be continued for any length of time in any other than a formal manner, requires, generally speaking, a measure of strength or godly desire. Therefore the time we can best perform this exercise of the soul is after the inner man has been nourished by meditation on the word of God," said George Müller in describing the important role meditation played in his life. "This is when we find the Father speaking to us, to encourage us, to comfort us, to instruct us, to humble us, or to reprove us."

As a woman today, however, it can be particularly difficult to find enough "alone time." How do we avoid being distracted as we quietly reflect on the Word of God? Being alone with the Lord is markedly different from fellowshiping with God in the presence of others. Yet the many dimensions of our lives contrive to crowd out our time with God. Or is that just an excuse we use?

George Müller would often go out into the fields and walk, taking his Bible and a special large-print New Testament. "I used to find the time spent in walking a loss," Müller confessed, "but now I find it very profitable, not only to my body, but also to my soul."

What a contrast this type of "fitness" program is to those promoted on the many exercise tapes and videos that are current best-sellers! By simply walking and talking alone with God, Bible in hand, Reverend Müller discovered the *real* meaning of "wellness": health that affects the whole person, body and soul, inside as well as out. Just like yoga and vegetarianism, today's glut of physical fitness regimens do absolutely nothing to improve the condition of our hearts before God.

Why not combine seeking with walking or swimming or cycling? The pursuit of godliness need not drive us to a monastery to produce lasting benefit. "Never wait for a fitter time or place to talk to Him," wrote George MacDonald. "To wait till thou go to church or to thy closet is to make Him wait. He will listen as thou walkest."

We can reap the fruit of fellowship with the Lord *wherever* and *whenever* we make the choice to set our minds upon His Word. *"You will seek me and find me when you seek me with all your heart,"* He promised (Jer. 29:13). He is waiting to meet us even now.

❧　❧　❧　❧　❧

Lord, when I slow my thoughts down
　long enough to partake
　　of Your life-giving Word,
　　　I taste eternal bounty.
You satisfy my hungry heart
　with Bread that springs to life
　　within me, as You give freely to all
　　　who long to eat from Your table.
I thank You for the feast
　You have prepared for me,

for the strength You alone
can give to Your loved ones.
In quietness and confidence,
let me learn to feed upon
the everlasting joy of Your presence
as I take delight in knowing You.

❦   ❦   ❦   ❦   ❦

Points to Ponder
—*THEME: Acts 17:16-33*

I can always tell when I've been too busy to draw near to the Lord because I _____
_____.

God's Word has a greater impact on me if I _____
_____
_____.

Spending time alone with God in order to know Him better is different from the time I spend in prayer because _____
_____
_____.

The greatest hindrance to my personal communion with God is _____
_____.

Meditation leads to prayer and praise when _____
_____
_____.

To avoid being distracted as I quietly reflect on the Word of God, I _____
_____.

Additional Study
—*MEDITATE ON* Psalm 105:1-4; 119:1-8, 97-104;
and 139.
—*READ ABOUT* an Old Testament woman, the Queen
of Sheba, in 2 Chronicles 9:1-12.
—*STUDY* 2 Peter 1:3-11; Ephesians 3:16-21; and
1 Chronicles 16:8-13.

—*MEMORIZE* Proverbs 8:17; Matthew 5:6; and
   Jeremiah 29:13.

❦ ❦ ❦ ❦ ❦

*Acquaint thyself with God, if thou would'st
taste His works. Admitted once to His
embrace, thou shalt perceive that thou wast
blind before: thine eye shall be instructed;
and thine heart made pure shall relish with
divine delight, till then unfelt, what hands
Divine have wrought.*

                    —WILLIAM COWPER
                    1731-1800

Praying

They all joined together constantly in prayer, along with the women and Mary the mother of Jesus, and with his brothers.
—ACTS 1:14

Prayer is a sincere, sensible, affectionate pouring out of the soul to God, through Christ in the strength and assistance of the Holy Spirit, for such things as God has promised.

In prayer it is better to have a heart without words than words without heart.
—JOHN BUNYAN
1628-1688

Prayer is not eloquence, but earnestness; not the definition of helplessness, but the feeling of it; not figures of speech, but earnestness of soul.
—HANNAH MORE
1745-1833

My prayers, my God, flow from what I am not; I think Thy answers make me what I am. Like weary waves thought follows upon thought. But the still depth beneath is all Thine own, And there Thou mov'st in paths to us unknown. Out of strange strife Thy peace is strangely wrought; If the lion in us pray—Thou answerest the lamb.
—GEORGE MACDONALD
1824-1905

"I lift up my eyes to the hills—where does my help come from?" asks the psalmist (Ps. 121:1). We can almost picture him looking back and forth across the horizon, scanning the rocks and trees and sky to locate the source of his sustenance. Nothing in creation, however, can supply what he needs: "My help," he confidently declares, "comes from the Lord, *the Maker* of heaven and earth" (v. 2).

Compare this response to a frequently heard declaration of independence voiced by so many women today: "I have the power to choose; I have the right to decide my own fate." Scores of self-help books lining the shelves of bookstores and hundreds of speakers on talk shows seem to endlessly repeat this refrain.

Yet those of us who identify with the words of the psalmist have come to realize that such information is severely limited. The cry of our hearts differs markedly from the chorus of our culture: "Help me, Lord!" whispers the woman who weeps over a troubled marriage; "Forgive me, Father," confesses the mother who has just exploded in anger at her two-year-old child; "Show me what to do, Jesus," pleads the teenage cheerleader pressured by her peers. Through simple prayers like these, women are daily discovering God's infinite strength and all-encompassing power.

Jesus taught that prayer centers first on the Creator, not the created; on the supernatural rather than the natural; on our heavenly Father instead of on ourselves. "Our Father in heaven, hallowed be *your* name, *your* kingdom come, *your* will be done on earth as it is in heaven," He prayed (Matt. 6:9-10). It is from this vantage point that our prayers are expressed as we, like the psalmist, recognize the true source of our help, strength, nourishment, and protection.

"The God we must learn to know," wrote A.W. Tozer, "is the Majesty in the heavens, the Father almighty, the Maker of heaven and earth, the only wise God our Savior."

In a very real sense, prayer opens our eyes to the state of God's creation. Through prayer, we acknowledge who we are before the Lord and seek to understand His will; we lift our eyes up "to the hills" to fix our attention on the direction our Father wants us to go, alerting us to the unseen realms of

God. This type of spiritual alertness is never an automatic reaction, especially when multiple distractions and worldly attitudes pull our thoughts back down to earth on a regular basis.

In his letter to the Ephesians, Paul uses such words as *plead, remind,* and *earnest* in regard to prayer, and in 6:18 he even admonishes believers to "pray all the time" (LB). To pray on all occasions requires vigilant attentiveness, dependence upon the Holy Spirit, and a continuing desire to look beyond the idols of this world to the eternal realities of God's kingdom.

Through a never-ceasing barrage of self-help messages, seductive images, and mood music, it is difficult to feel the urgency to which Paul was referring. We have few role models, if any, in the public eye who are known for praying fervently on behalf of God's creation. But behind closed doors, in the quiet privacy of their homes and Bible studies and churches, countless women are encountering the powerful reality of prayer. At kitchen sinks, over telephone lines, and beside dining room tables the most valuable hidden resource of this nation is lifted above the din of our culture to reach the throne room of heaven. Without recognition, women who are dedicating their lives to the purposes of God are becoming increasingly more cognizant of God's sovereignty, omnipotence, and compassion.

Of all the women in the Bible, the group of women from Galilee who followed Jesus were the most closely associated with the Lord. Yet we rarely read stories about them. They are not even referred to by name for the most part. Like so many of God's praying people today, these women seem almost anonymous to us. What distinguishes them from other women in the New Testament is the frequency with which they appear at key moments in Scripture and the activities in which they were faithfully involved.

Luke 8:2 tells us that these women had been set free from evil spirits and diseases, that they traveled with Jesus and His disciples and supported them out of their own means. In Luke 23 we see that they witnessed Christ's crucifixion and burial, and in the following chapter learn that they prepared spices for Jesus' body and discovered His empty tomb. One of their number, Mary of Magdala, was even privileged to be greeted by the risen Lord—the first person to have received this honor—and was given the word of His resurrection to carry to the disciples.

Then in Acts 1:14 we hear of these women once more. On this occasion they had joined the disciples in the Upper Room to await the baptism of the Holy Spirit following Christ's ascension into heaven. Their primary activity? *Constant prayer.*

❦   ❦   ❦   ❦   ❦

The women had followed Him
    from the town of Galilee—
Mary of Magdala,
    Joanna,
        Salome,
            Susanna,
                and Mary, His mother.
Different ages,
    different backgrounds—
a wide assortment of women
    who had heard the Master's call—
one a former slave to demons,
    another a royal manager's wife.
Younger women,
    older women,
married women,
    single women,
all joined together
    by their faith in Jesus,
all responding to
    the same clear message:
"Do not leave Jerusalem, but wait."

Only prayer could have kept them
    going strong;
only prayer could have brought
    peace and perspective
        after weeks of witnessing

their risen Lord,
then hearing His final word:
wait.

How could they have known
what they were waiting *for*?
How do *we* know
what we are waiting for?
How can we ever presume to know
what God will do?

❧   ❧   ❧   ❧   ❧

Considering the Challenge
"They all joined together constantly in prayer."

"Those who have left the deepest impression on this sin-cursed earth have been men and women of prayer," wrote D.L. Moody, evangelist and founder of Moody Bible Institute. "You will find that PRAYER has been the mighty power that has moved not only God, but man."

In my own life, learning how to pray has been a growth process in response to the Lord working upon my mind and heart. Certainly answered prayer has been an encouragement in this direction; but even more important has been the growth of my desire to pray as my love for the Lord has deepened. When I am confronted by the magnitude of what it means to live in a fallen world, to live within the weakness of human flesh, prayer becomes my most vital link to HOME. Requests for help, confessions of homesickness, tales of life on the road, urgent pleas for specific needs: these are the things that follow my declarations of love and appreciation for my heavenly Father.

In his classic book *How to Pray*, R.A. Torrey said that to be effective, prayer "should really be *unto God*...a definite and conscious approach to God...a definite and vivid realization that God is bending over us and listening as we pray." Instead, he said, "In very much of our prayer there is really but little thought of God. Our mind is taken up with the thought of what we need, and is not occupied with the thought of the mighty and loving Father of whom we are seeking it.

"Oftentimes...we are occupied neither with the need nor with the One to whom we are praying, but our mind is wandering here and there throughout the world. There is no power in that sort of prayer. But when we really come into God's presence, really meet Him face to face in the place of prayer, really seek the things that we desire *from Him,* then there is power."

Longing for the Lord and the reality of His kingdom lies at the root of all effective prayer. Though our minds are easily distracted from this pursuit, the Holy Spirit helps us in our weakness, interceding "with groans that words cannot express" (Rom. 8:26). We must willingly cooperate with the Spirit, praying with our whole heart—secretly, fervently, singlemindedly—if we want to experience the blessings of godliness. No other activity brings us closer to participating alongside the Lord on behalf of His creation.

❧   ❧   ❧   ❧   ❧

> Prayer is the soul's sincere desire,
>   Uttered or unexpressed;
> The motion of a hidden fire,
>   That trembles in the breast.
>
> Prayer is the burden of a sigh,
>   The falling of a tear;
> The upward glancing of an eye,
>   When none but God is near.
>
> Prayer is the simplest form of speech
>   That infant lips can try;
> Prayer, the sublimest strains that reach
>   The Majesty on high.
>
> Prayer is the contrite sinner's voice,
>   Returning from his ways;
> While angels in their songs rejoice,
>   And cry, "Behold! He prays!"

Prayer is the Christian's vital breath,
    The Christian's native air;
His watchword at the gate of death—
    He enters heaven with prayer.

The saints in prayer appear as one
    In word and deed and mind;
Where with the Father and the Son
    Sweet fellowship they find.

No prayer is made by man alone:
    The Holy Spirit pleads;
And Jesus, on eternal Throne,
    For sinners intercedes.

O Thou by whom we come to God—
    The Life, the Truth, the Way!
The path of prayer Thyself hast trod;
    Lord, teach us how to pray!
                 —JAMES MONTGOMERY
                 1771-1854

❧   ❧   ❧   ❧   ❧

Considering the Challenge
    "Your kingdom come, your will be done."

Have you often wanted to spend time praying but ended up daydreaming or dozing off instead? (Do I hear anyone else answering this question *honestly*?) Do you find yourself frequently becoming distracted, interrupted, or otherwise dissuaded from spending more than five or ten minutes at a time in prayer? (You too?) What is the secret to engaging wholeheartedly in hour-long or day-long prayer times? (No, the answer is *not* "Enter a convent!")

    "Any housewife knows that the best way to remember the things she meant to do and forgot is to start praying," said Vance Havner. "They will come to her and divert her from prayer. The devil will let a preacher prepare a sermon if it will keep him from preparing himself."

Seriously, no matter how persistent or constant we are in our prayer life, we all need help at times to keep us from being distracted. Some of these are practical helps such as praying aloud to keep our minds from wandering, kneeling so that we stay alert, shutting off the phone so we aren't interrupted, or making a list of needs to refer to as reminders as we pray. However, we need another and more powerful source of help also, and that is the help of the Holy Spirit.

Jesus sends the Holy Spirit into our lives to prepare our hearts to know how and when to pray. Our part is to be attentive, watchful, ready, and obedient to turn our thoughts toward the thoughts of God. Praying in accord with the Holy Spirit depends primarily upon our eagerness and willingness to participate in prayer and cannot—must not—rely on mere "head knowledge" alone.

"As the Spirit breathes out the 'Father' cry of a child, which is the prayer-cry, so He helps us in our praying.... He is the master-prayer," writes S.D. Gordon in *Quiet Talks on Prayer.* "He knows God's will perfectly. He knows what best to be praying in all circumstances. And He is within you and me.... He prompts us to pray. He calls us to the quiet room to our knees. He inclines to prayer wherever we are."

As you wait upon the Lord to prepare your heart, ask Him for the power of concentration. Pull your thoughts back from daydreaming, fixing your attention on a portion of God's Word. For example, "Search me, O God, and know my heart; test me and know my anxious thoughts," might be a helpful starting point (Ps. 139:23). Reach out for all the Lord has for you! Don't be content with less. Wait on the Lord: upon His presence, upon His cleansing. Worship Him with reverence and awe. Taste and see the goodness of your Maker. *Then* prayer will become a cooperative effort and a time of rich blessing as the Holy Spirit enables you to pray effectively, articulately, and with heartfelt compassion.

"The greatest prayer any one of us can offer is, 'Thy will be done.' It will be offered in a thousand different forms, with a thousand different details, as needs arise daily. But every true prayer comes under those words," says Gordon. But, he warns, "There might be a false submission to his supposed will in some affliction; a not reaching out to *all* He has for us."

91

Jesus spent entire nights praying. On three different occasions Moses spent forty days and nights alone with God. David, Daniel, and the Lord Jesus practiced a "morning watch" for the purpose of meditation upon the Word of God and prayer (Ps. 5:3; Dan. 6:10; Mark 1:35). Setting aside specific time to pray is a sacrifice we can't afford *not* to make.

Given the scope of prayer—what prayer throughout history has accomplished—we have every reason to "approach the throne of grace with confidence, so that we may receive mercy and find grace to help us in our time of need" (Heb. 4:16). Because the Holy Spirit will help us and intercede for us, we can be confident that our prayers are an effective and powerful tool against the devil's schemes.

❦   ❦   ❦   ❦   ❦

Lord, even though I know
that praying is a privilege,
    an art to be nurtured,
        a gift to be shared,
I often do not listen
    to Your still small voice.
I madly rush
    from one place to another
as if blinded by the things I see
    or deafened by the things I hear.
My mind is filled
    with the strangest things!
The fragments of my life
    are an oddball asssortment
    of bits and pieces,
        all thrown together
        and jumbled like scraps of fabric
            left over from a recent sewing project.
Praying sorts the pieces out
    one at a time.
As I give my life to You,
    You design a quilt more lovely
        than anything put together
            by human hands.

Your pattern always reveals
    the wisdom of Your design—
Your trademark can be found
    in each reconstructed life
        You tenderly fashion.

I thank You for avoiding
    an assembly-line approach
        to my pain and my questions,
    for loving me enough
        to answer my prayers
        individually.
I marvel at Your ability to listen,
    to bend low to hear me
        when I call Your name.

Help me, heavenly Father, to pray more often,
    to devote my heart
        to drawing near to You.
Strengthen my capacity
    to believe.
I love You, Lord, and praise You
    for all that You have done
        and all that You are doing
           and all that You will continue to do.

❦   ❦   ❦   ❦   ❦

Points to Ponder
    —*THEME: Acts 1:12-14; Matthew 6:5-13*

The more I pray, the more I _____
_____
_____.
Prayer is _____
_____.
I am encouraged to pray when _____
_____
_____.
My prayer life would benefit from _____

_____
_____ .
From Jesus' prayer life we can learn _____
_____
_____ .
I could become more involved in praying with and for others
by _____
_____ .
When I pray in private, I am hindered by things like _____
_____
_____ .

Additional Study

— *MEDITATE ON* Psalms 3, 34, 61, and 142.
— *READ ABOUT* an Old Testament woman, Hannah, in
   1 Samuel 1.
— *STUDY* 1 Thessalonians 5:16-18; Romans 8:22-27;
   James 5:13-18.
— *MEMORIZE* Psalm 141:1-2 and Matthew 26:41.

❧   ❧   ❧   ❧   ❧

*Real prayer is a serious concern, for we are
speaking to the Sovereign Lord of all the
universe, who is willing to move heaven and
earth in answer to sincere and reasonable
prayer. Prayer is not a mechanical duty, but
a wonderful opportunity to develop a loving
and caring relationship with the most
important Person in our lives.*
— JOHN BUNYAN

Praising

*My soul glorifies the Lord
and my spirit rejoices in God my Savior...
for the Mighty One has done great
things for me—
holy is his name.*
        —LUKE 1:46, 49

We celebrate not our sickness but our cure.
        —SAINT GREGORY

*What should we set as our ultimate goal in
this life? The answer: the most perfect
worshippers of God we can possibly be,
like we hope to be throughout eternity.*
— BROTHER LAWRENCE
1611-1691

*In heaven we will praise God "face to face."
The current of song will pour straight
from us to him. But we need not wait
until then. We can start the singing
early.*
— TIM STAFFORD

*When God is the center of your life, you
can praise Him every day, because you
will always find blessings no matter how
difficult your circumstances. To a praising saint, the circumstances of life are a
window through which he sees God.*
— WARREN WIERSBE

The sound of music follows us everywhere—in the shopping mall and the supermarket, in the hair salon and the shoe store, in the elevator and at the dentist. But the melodies that accompany us on our daily errands are not by Mozart or Beethoven; instead, they pour forth in a continual stream of instrumental "musak" from the repetoires of Frank Sinatra, Olivia Newton-John, Neil Diamond, and the like. Designed for businesses for the purpose of relaxing customers, these notes resound persistently, even on telephone "hold" lines and in hospital corridors. We can't escape the sound; yet it has become so much a part of our environment that most of the time we are not even aware of it.

Then, in late November, a strange phenomenon occurs: we begin to notice the music more as we hear strains of Handel and Mendelssohn and Bach announcing the arrival of the Christmas season with "Joy to the World," "Hark the Herald Angels Sing," and "Jesu, Joy of Man's Desiring." For a brief time each year these sound systems play music that was written in praise to God. Ironically, if it were any other time, customers and clients would probably complain and the ACLU would be up in arms!

The sounds of our culture—media broadcasting, background music, and city noises—can have a numbing, anesthetic effect on our awareness of the Lord's presence. Unlike the birds, who sing their soaring melodies of thanksgiving in nearly any environment, we are apt to become absentminded and complacent about expressing our own unique songs of praise.

"How good it is to sing praises to our God, how pleasant and fitting to praise him!" declares the psalmist in Psalm 147 (v. 1). Perhaps the birds realize this better than we do. "The joy of birds is one of the most wonderful things about them," wrote Amy Carmichael. "They seem to sing from the moment they awake, even if they are awakened by cold wind and rain. They sing before they set to work to find something to eat. And not one is forgotten by God who knows all the birds of the sky."

We praise God by choice, not instinct. To shake off our numbness and complacency we must view praise as a daily gift to the Lord rather than just an occasional duty. "The God of the joy of birds," Miss Carmichael reminds us, "wants our joy too." Are we willing to tune out the droning distractions of our culture and enter His courts with praise? To sing the choruses of Christmas even in the midst of the sticky heat of July?

"Let the word of Christ dwell in you richly...as you sing psalms, hymns and spiritual songs with gratitude in your hearts to God," Paul told the Colossians (3:16). Through praise, we recognize who God is and communicate our reverence for Him. Through praise, we lift our voices to the One who has made us in His image, using words to describe His infinite majesty, glory, and power. Through praise, we look toward Christ as the Lamb seated on the throne, the Victor who has vanquished the enemy, the Lover awaiting His beloved. Just as music comes in many forms, so our praises can be declarations...proclamations...and even love songs, all year long!

When Mary went to visit Zechariah and Elizabeth in Judea, her response to Elizabeth's joyous welcome was a spontaneous burst of praise and worship. As you read Luke 1:39-56, consider the strength and beauty with which this young woman praised God as she lifted her voice as a fragrant offering to the Lord.

❦ ❦ ❦ ❦ ❦

My soul glorifies the Lord
and my spirit rejoices
in God my Savior....

O Lord! I understand who You are!
A mighty God—
so holy,
merciful,
and victorious!

You are my King,
my Lord,
my Savior.

You bring salvation
from on high!
So wonderfully
You have dealt with me;
so tenderly
You have looked upon
Your servant.
My spirit rejoices
in You, Most High God!
Your name is holy,
Your mercy endures forever,
Your deeds are righteous!
The humble You have lifted high
and the hungry You have satisfied
with good things.

O rejoice,
rejoice,
my spirit,
in God my Savior.
Bless the Lord, my soul;
my innermost heart,
bless His holy name!

❦   ❦   ❦   ❦   ❦

Considering the Challenge
"Through Jesus, therefore, let us continually
offer to God a sacrifice of praise..." (Heb. 13:15).

Praising our Creator can mean bowing low in humility or
singing out to Him enthusiastically. Praise is *an offering* to
the Most High God in thankful recognition of His absolute
holiness and divinity. True praise runs counter to everything
in us that prefers to exalt self above God; thus, praise can only
arise from our willingness to take our eyes off ourselves and
turn our thoughts toward our Father in heaven.

"Worship is the highest and noblest act that any person
can do," says Raymond C. Ortlund. "When [you] worship,
God is satisfied! 'The Father seeketh such to worship Him.'

Amazing, isn't it? And when you worship, you are fulfilled! Think about this: why did Jesus Christ come? He came to make worshippers out of rebels. We who were once completely self-centered have to be completely changed so that we can shift our attention outside of ourselves and become able to worship Him."

Worshipers out of rebels...saints out of sinners. This realization calls to my mind Paul's exuberant declaration of praise. "Oh, the depth of the riches of the wisdom and knowledge of God! How unsearchable his judgments, and his paths beyond tracing out! Who has known the mind of the Lord? Or who has been his counselor? Who has ever given to God, that God should repay him? For from him and through him and to him are all things. To him be the glory forever! Amen" (Rom. 11:33-36).

What a privilege it is to be part of such a heritage as we lift up the name of the Lord and worship as members of His family. We are no longer strangers to the kingdom of God, but can sing praise to our holy King with the angels.

      ❧   ❧   ❧   ❧   ❧

Fill Thou my life, O Lord my God,
In every part with praise,
That my whole being may proclaim
Thy being and Thy ways.

Not for the lip of praise alone,
Nor for the praising heart—
I ask Thee for a life made up
Of praise in every part.

Praise in the common things of life,
Its goings out and in;
Praise in each duty and each deed,
However small and mean.

Fill every part of me with praise:
Let all my being speak
Of Thee and of Thy love, O Lord,
Poor though I be, and weak.

So shalt Thou, Lord, from even me
Receive Thy glory due;
And so shall I begin on earth
The song forever new.

So shall no part of day or night
From sacredness be free;
But all my life, in every step,
Be fellowship with Thee.

— HORATIUS BONAR
1808-1889

❧   ❧   ❧   ❧   ❧

Putting It Into Practice

"...the fruit of lips that confess his name" (Heb.13:15).

"Praise of God is fundamental to my relationship with him," writes Tim Stafford in *Knowing the Face of God*. "It opens a channel of loving regard. When I bring my requests to God, I stand by him looking toward mutual concerns, but when I praise him my eyes are lifted in intimacy and warmth toward him. I look to his face.... Praise makes me vulnerable. When I praise, I take off the mask of the hardened critic and expose myself as an ardent fan and lover."

Does this sound like something that would be comfortable for the "self" conscious person? There is no doubt that in today's world it is all too easy to be self-conscious and aware of those around us, even during worship. We worry about how we look or whether we will impress others. Yet the Lord is concerned with the attitude of our heart.

Remember David's act of worship as he "danced before the Lord with all his might" while the Ark of the Covenant was being brought into Jerusalem (2 Sam. 6:12-23)? As his wife Michal watched from a window, she despised David for leaping and dancing about the streets of the city in such an undignified manner, in full view of his subjects and servants. Michal was concerned only with her husband's outward appearance, whereas God looked upon David's heart.

What lesson can we learn from this story? Is such behavior pleasing to the Lord even today—or is it strictly off-limits?

The art of praise, Stafford suggests, "is not to out-emote others, to raise our hands higher, to dance with more reckless abandon, to roll our eyes or clap our hands. *The art is to get our eyes off ourselves so we do not care how we look....* My posture—kneeling or closing my eyes or opening them to look at a cross or raising my hands—may help me. A piece of music, especially a well-loved familiar one, may help. What helps one person will not help another.... Ultimately we must not only say or sing certain 'praise' words or adopt a certain 'praise' posture or feel certain 'praise' feelings; *we must focus on God and do it before him.* Why? Because the goal of praise is not an experience; it is a relationship. The best aids to worship are those that because of their simplicity or familiarity become clear as glass. We do not see them at all; we see through them to the Lord."

The point of praise is never ourselves; it is always the object of our praise, the Lord. *Lifting our eyes in intimacy and warmth, or in exuberant celebration, toward our Maker...continually offering a sacrifice of praise to God.* "I will praise you, O Lord, with all my heart; I will tell of all your wonders. I will be glad and rejoice in you; I will sing praise to your name, O Most High" (Ps. 9:1-2).

❦   ❦   ❦   ❦   ❦

O Lord, how vast,
   how immeasurable,
     how unfathomable
       You are!
You are in me and around me.
Throughout Your creation,
You bring all things together
     perfectly.
It is beyond my understanding—
   I thank You and praise You,
     Heavenly Father,
for Your mercy and grace,
   Your patience and forgiveness,
     Your righteousness and truth.
Let there be honor and glory

to Your name forever!
All praise to the Lamb
  who was slain
    so that I might live!
Those You have rescued from the darkness
    REJOICE!
I kneel before
    my risen Lord
        in homage to my King.
May the songs I sing
    and the sacrifice I bring
be pleasing and acceptable in Your sight,
    both now and forevermore.

❦ ❦ ❦ ❦ ❦

Points to Ponder
—THEME: *Luke 1:39-56*

Like prayer, praise is a privilege to be practiced with _____
_____
_____.

It seems most natural for me to praise God when _____
_____
_____.

I find myself praising God when _____
_____
_____.

I think I could learn to praise more expressively and creatively
by _____
_____.

Of all the descriptions of people praising God in the Bible, I
especially enjoy _____
_____.

Praise is portrayed as a sacrifice because _____
_____
_____.

Praise can be a comfort in time of sorrow or crisis because
_____
_____.

103

Additional Study

— *MEDITATE ON* Psalms 95, 96, 148, and 150.
— *READ ABOUT* an Old Testament woman, Hannah,
   in 1 Samuel 1:24—2:10.
— *STUDY* 1 Peter 1:3-9; Ephesians 1:3-14; and
   1 Chronicles 15:25—16:36.
—*MEMORIZE* 1 Peter 2:9; Colossians 3:16; and
   Psalm 147:1.

❧ ❧ ❧ ❧ ❧

HOLY FATHER,
I have been treading on holy ground!
Who would dare to contemplate the wonder
of God! Who would dare to listen to the
worshiping hosts
   in heaven around Your holy throne!
Father, I confess that You are wonderful,
   in all that You are,
   in all that You do,
   in all that You say to me in Your Word.
I see now how far short I have come
      in my personal worship—
      how much I have to learn.
Be patient with me!
Receive my worship, my praise, my thanks-
giving, through Jesus Christ my Lord.
AMEN.

—WARREN WIERSBE

PART THREE

Reflections on Serving God

> Consecrate yourselves and be holy,
> because I am the Lord your God.
> Keep my decrees and follow them.
> I am the Lord, who makes you holy.
> —LEVITICUS 20:7-8

O Breath of Life, come sweeping through us,
  Revive Your Church with life and power;
O Breath of Life, come, cleanse, renew us,
  And fit Your Church to meet this hour.

O Wind of God, come bend us, break us,
  'Til humbly we confess our need;
Then in Your tenderness remake us,
  Revive, restore—for this we plead.

O Breath of Love, come breathe within us,
  Renewing thought and will and heart;
Come, Love of Christ, afresh to win us,
  Revive Your Church in every part.

O Heart of Christ, once broken for us,
  In You we find our strength and rest;
Our broken contrite hearts now solace,
  And let Your waiting Church be blest.

Revive us, Lord! Is zeal abating
While harvest fields are vast and white?
Revive us, Lord—the world is waiting!
Equip Your Church to spread the light.
    —Bessie Porter Head

Sharing

*In Joppa there was a disciple named
Tabitha (which, when translated, is
Dorcas), who was always doing good
and helping the poor.*
    —ACTS 9:36

*You must live with people in order
to know their problems, and live
with God in order to solve them.*
    —P.T. FORSYTH

*It is of no avail to talk of the church
in general, the church in the abstract,
unless the concrete particular local
church which people attend can become
a center of light and leading, of
inspiration and guidance, for its
specific community.*
 —RUFUS JONES
  1863-1948

*We, you and I, form the primary
representation of God's presence
in the world. What is God like?
Where does he live? How can the
world get to know him? His presence
no longer dwells in a tabernacle
in Sinai, or in a temple in Jerusalem.
He has chosen, instead, to dwell
in ordinary, even ornery, people like
you and me.*
 —PHILIP YANCEY

"Nothing could more surely convince me of God's unending mercy than the continued existence on earth of the church," states writer Annie Dillard. Stop and think about the implications of this statement. What is the church? Certainly it's more than a building and more than the clergy. The church is made up of people. Not just spiritual giants like Peter and Paul and Mary of Magdala, but people like you and me. "We, you and I, form the primary representation of God's presence in the world," says writer Philip Yancey. Gulp. What an awesome thought! But there's just no getting around it: the church—the body of Christ—lives, acts, testifies, and loves through you and me.

"You are Christ's body, and each of you a limb or an organ in it," proclaims Paul (1 Cor. 12:27 NEB), using the graphic metaphor of the body found repeatedly in the Word of God. Thus, we each have a special function within the body of the Lord, and it is essential that we recognize this and genuinely respect one another's differences.

How can I possibly do my job as a hand or a foot or an elbow if I am constantly comparing myself with a wrist or a leg or a forearm? To share my gift wholeheartedly, out of obedience to the Lord and love for His body, I must work in harmony with others as well as develop and use the gifts God has given to me.

In a sense, nothing could seem more foreign than this kind of intimate cooperation in our busy, self-centered society. Raised in isolation from those outside our immediate families, we find it tremendously challenging to even open up our homes and our lives to other members of the body of Christ. It's much more comfortable to stay safely in the shelter of our own familiar environments! But the church is neither risk-free nor pain-free. It requires the sweat of corporate discipline, the effort of personal sacrifice.

Just as our bodies weaken without use, so the body of Christ loses its strength when not actively "exercised" by its members. Functioning in a coordinated, well-structured manner requires training, practice, maintenance, and commitment to sticking with the program. We will suffer bumps and bruises. We will feel like giving up at times. We will occasionally wonder if we are ever going to cross the finish line intact. But much of what Jesus talked about—sharing, serving, submitting, persevering, and loving—relates to the very things that tend to make us stumble. He never promised us it was going to be comfortable. Or automatic. Or fast.

The women from Galilee described in Luke 8:1-3 and Dorcas in Acts 9:36-43 are powerful examples of what it means to share one's gifts as part of the body of Christ. The level of commitment of these women in the early church made a significant difference in the work of God's kingdom, but it cost them time and talent and money and personal involvement.

So often we want to hold back in one or all of these areas; we don't want to *share* ourselves. As you read about these women, reflect on how their capacity to yield their lives to Christ illustrates what it means to be a fragrant offering.

❧　❧　❧　❧　❧

Out of their own means ....
　　Always doing good ....
Did they wonder what they had to share,
　　or did they just begin by sharing
　　　　what they had?
Did they worry about what others would think,
　　or did they think about others
　　　　instead of themselves?
Did they give cheerfully because it was easier,
　　or was it easier to be cheerful
　　　　because they gave?
Did they wait for the perfect time to be obedient,
　　or was the Lord's timing perfect
　　　　whenever they obeyed?

Follow me
　　implies action
　　　　instead of hesitation;
　　moving forward
　　　　instead of standing still;

changes in scenery
    instead of predictable surroundings.

You have called us to follow You, Lord,
    as we do the work of Your kingdom
    here and now.
When we share with Your body,
    we show others what You can do
        and tell them that You did not
            leave us behind
                to do the work alone.

By Your Spirit may we learn to
    act
        move
            change
                function
                    and grow
    as Your body—
        no longer separate,
            but *one!*

❦   ❦   ❦   ❦   ❦

Considering the Challenge
"Be patient, bearing with one another in love."
—EPHESIANS 4:2

Have you ever gotten so fed up with believers in your church that you withdrew from them, physically or emotionally? Has having to share with the body of Christ made you more aware of your natural tendencies to be self-centered and competitive?

Only by responding to the supernatural love produced by the Holy Spirit are we able to live in harmony with one another. Often it all boils down to being able to say, "I'm sorry" (and really mean it!) and to forgive those who have wronged or offended us. Although this sounds simple, it isn't.

"Confession is very out of fashion today," believes Dick

Keyes. "This has something to do with today's values and lifestyle, but at a deeper level, confession has never been in fashion. It is always hard to do." True confession and forgiveness are central to our ability to share with other believers. But if we are honest, we must admit that we find it much more comfortable to hide from one another—and from God—when we feel inadequate or angry or ashamed.

Can you imagine how different churches would be today if we became truly confessional toward one another? If we gave up hiding? If we acknowledged once and for all that we all fall short when it comes to loving one another the way Jesus would have us love? Although it is scary, the practice of confession and forgiveness is the Lord's own prescription for knocking down the walls that prevent meaningful sharing. The first step is to begin with those closest to us—in our home and friendships—and then extend the circle outward.

"Forgiveness is the key to action and freedom," wrote Hannah Arendt. "Without it life is governed by an endless cycle of resentment and retaliation."

"If I am not willing to say, 'I'm sorry,' when I have wronged somebody else—especially when I have not loved him—I have not even started to think about the meaning of a Christian oneness which the world can see," declares Francis Schaeffer in *The Mark of the Christian*. "The world has a right to question whether I am a Christian. And more than that...if I am not willing to do this very simple thing, the world has a right to question whether Jesus was sent from God and whether Christianity is true."

Schaeffer then asks: "How well have we consciously practiced this? How often, in the power of the Holy Spirit, have we gone to Christians in our own group and said, 'I'm sorry'?" Loving one another in ways that the world can observe means loving one another *"in the midst of our differences,"* he concludes: loving *"when it costs us something,"* loving *"even under times of tremendous emotional tension."* In other words, loving one another *"in a way the world can see."*

The apostle Paul gave the secret of this loving unity to the Ephesians: "Be completely humble and gentle; be patient, bearing with one another in love. Make every effort to keep the unity of the Spirit through the bond of peace. There is one body and one Spirit—just as you were called to one hope when you were called—one Lord, one faith, one baptism; one God and Father of all, who is over all and through all and in all" (Eph. 4:2-6).

Genuine Christian sharing within the body of Christ requires humility, gentleness, patience—all the results of "bearing with one another in love." Without love, we can never speak to a dying world about what it means to be the body of Christ or about who Jesus really is. Love must guide and fill and complete our sharing in ways that the world can see.

❧ ❧ ❧ ❧ ❧

> We give Thee but Thine own,
> Whate'er the gift may be:
> All that we have is Thine alone,
> A trust, O Lord, from Thee.
>
> May we Thy bounties thus
> As stewards true receive,
> And gladly as Thou blessest us,
> To Thee our first-fruits give.
>
> To comfort and to bless,
> To find a balm for woe,
> To tend the lone and fatherless,
> Is angels' work below.
>
> The captive to release,
> To God the lost to bring,
> To teach the way of life and peace,
> It is a Christ-like thing.
>
> And we believe Thy word,
> Though dim our faith may be,
> Whate'er for Thine we do, O Lord,
> We do it unto Thee.
>
> —WILLIAM WALSHAM HOW
> *1823-1897*

❧ ❧ ❧ ❧ ❧

Putting It Into Practice
"Live a life worthy of the calling you have received."

I love to buy gifts for people. In fact, I find it as much fun as buying something for myself. As I select a gift, I think about the person, what she is like, what colors she prefers, what interests she has—and I try to find something she might not buy for herself. In other words, a gift is something very special and very individual, chosen with just one person in mind.

God's gifts are like that, too. I marvel at His capacity for endless variations on a theme; no two women are exactly the same. The challenge for me is not to look at Lori or Linda or Shawn or Susan and think to myself, Why is it she can do that so well and I can't? Instead, I try to remind myself often of the words of Dag Hammarskjold: "Humility means not to compare." God chooses the gifts He gives us wisely, lovingly, with His purposes in mind. I need to believe that about my friends. (I need to believe that about myself, too!)

"All of us have gifts," writes Dick Keyes in *Beyond Identity*. "It might be the gift of building a building, nurturing a relationship, healing a body, or teaching a class. Our gifts extend across the whole range of human culture. We need to know what we are and are not good at. Here the church can be a great help by challenging people to see the diversity of their gifts and helping them to express them both within the church and in the culture at large."

Have you asked God to show you what your gifts are? Are you able to rest securely in the knowledge that you were not created to be all things to all people, but that you have a *specific* purpose to fulfill in the church? Isn't this exciting? Understanding that we each have something unique to contribute enables us to more deeply appreciate one another's differences, as well as our similarities.

There is a catch, however, warns Keyes: "In all of this, of course, we must not forget the danger of rooting our identity in gifts, jobs, achievements, or roles in society. God is at the center. Our identity is in him."

Our talents, our work, and our accomplishments are to

116

fit together with the lives of other believers in the local church in such a way that Christ's character is exhibited before a watching world. In this way, we share the gifts and the love God has given us for His honor and glory.

❧   ❧   ❧   ❧   ❧

Lord, Your Word reminds me
    that what I say
    and what I do
        matter.
When I share,
    I share You.
When I speak,
    I speak of You.
When I love,
    I love through You.
I am part of Your body,
    sharing and
        speaking and
            loving—
    whether I am weak or strong,
        healthy or afflicted,
            or just plain tired.
I am related to others in Your body
    not by common interests
        or genetic inheritance
            or denominational affiliation,
    but by Your blood.
By Your blood, You have shared
    everything that was needed
        to cancel my sin and
            make me one with them.
Open my eyes so that I might know
    what it means to love You, Lord,
        wherever You have placed me
            within Your body.

❧   ❧   ❧   ❧   ❧

Points to Ponder
— THEME: *Luke 8:1-3 and Acts 9:36-43*

Sharing myself and my gifts with others in the body of Christ is costly because _____ _____ _____.

Knowing my Father has created me to be a unique individual with talents to use on His behalf makes me realize _____ _____ _____.

When I compare myself with others, I often feel _____ _____ _____.

The next time I run into conflict with someone in my church, I will _____ _____ _____.

I can express my love for Jesus toward His body by _____ _____ _____.

I find it difficult to put love into action by saying "I'm sorry" because _____ _____ _____.

Additional Study

- — MEDITATE ON Psalms 133 and 135.
- — READ ABOUT an Old Testament woman, the widow of Zarephath, in 1 Kings 17:1-24.
- — STUDY Romans 12; 1 Corinthians 12:12-27; and Ephesians 4:1-16.
- — MEMORIZE John 13:34-35; Hebrews 9:14; and 1 Peter 4:8-11.

❧   ❧   ❧   ❧   ❧

Give me, good Lord, an humble, lowly,
quiet, peaceable, patient, charitable, kind,
and filial and tender mind, every shade,
in fact, of charity, with all my words and
all my works, and all my thoughts, to have
a taste of Thy holy blessed spirit.

—SIR THOMAS MORE

1478-1535

Serving

"I am the Lord's servant," Mary answered.
—LUKE 1:38

The world cannot always understand
one's profession of faith, but it can
understand service.
—IAN MACLAREN
1850-1907

If we look at our life as some precious treasure we must hoard, the demands made by others of our life are like losses.... But if we look at our life as a treasure we must share, every service we give to others is a fulfillment of our life's purpose.
— EDICIO DE LA TORRE

The person who looks for quick results in the seed-planting of well-doing will be disappointed. If I want potatoes for dinner tomorrow, it will do me little good to plant them in my garden tonight. There are long stretches of darkness and invisibility and silence that separate planting and reaping. During the stretches of waiting, there is cultivating and weeding and nurturing and planting still other seeds.
— EUGENE PETERSON

ights. Privileges. Opportunities. Ambition.
Success. These are common words in our
vocabulary. Perhaps more than at any other
time or place in history, people today expect comfort in every
area of life: physically, socially, emotionally, and economically.
Our society has taught us to aim for "the top." Even on a
spiritual level, millions of Americans seek comfortable solutions to the perplexities and problems of life. It is far easier to
sit and chant a mantra than to visit the dying in a nursing
home.

Perhaps the most striking and highly visible example of
privilege and comfort on view today is Great Britain's royal
family. Although there are many wealthy people, including
Americans, who have more money and greater power than
Queen Elizabeth and Prince Charles, they cannot buy a royal
title. Monarchy is transferred through bloodlines, not bank
accounts. In the economy of God, however, a completely
different value system was established when Jesus declared
that we achieve honor through *service*.

"In the Kingdom of God," writes T.W. Manson in *The
Church's Ministry,* "service is not a stepping-stone to nobility;
it *is* nobility, the only kind of nobility that is recognized."
Rank and status are determined by the attitude of our hearts
and the expression of our love for the Lord through our
humble service for Him.

"In all this emphasis on service, the disciple is only seeking to follow and reflect his teacher, for though he was Lord
of all Jesus became the servant of all," declares theologian
John Stott. "Putting on the apron of servitude, he got down
on his knees to wash the apostles' feet. Now he tells us to do
as he did, to clothe ourselves in humility, and in love to serve
one another."

Unless our hearts are softened and made more pliable by
God's love, we may find ourselves serving on the outside but
maintaining an attitude of pride on the inside. Arrogant servants cannot touch the hearts of others; in fact, they tend to
do just the opposite.

On the other hand, as children of God we can serve Him
wholeheartedly as members of His household because we
know we have *already* been promised our inheritance in the

kingdom of heaven. Then our service becomes a joyful response to the gift we have received by grace; we are simply showing our gratitude by following the example of our Brother. Serving the Lord with thanksgiving powerfully portrays to the world that we have accepted a different value system, that we believe our worth is not defined by our material possessions or our career success.

"A woman of excellence is one who has found her security and worth in Jesus Christ," says author Cynthia Heald. "Because of God's lovingkindness, His sovereignty, and His provision, she does not have to look to people or things to feel of value or loved. She is now free to love and serve because she can trust her needs to be met by her heavenly Father."

In the story of the Incarnation we find a young woman faced with the most extraordinary opportunity to serve God ever offered any woman in all of history. What an example Mary has set to inspire us to accept the will of God! As you read Luke 1:26-38, reflect upon the level of trust the Lord required of this remarkable woman for the remainder of her life.

❦   ❦   ❦   ❦   ❦

Rights? Privileges?
Opportunities?
Ambition? Success?
"Greetings, you who are highly favored!
The Lord is with you...."
(What higher honor than this?
What greater event than *the Word made flesh?*)

Confusion, mixed with fear and trembling!
What could this possibly mean?
What about Joseph? My family?
What about my future?
What will people think?
What is God doing to my life?

Realization, mixed with awe and wonder!
Yes, Lord, I love You!

I am Your servant!
*May it be to me
as You have said.*

*Nothing is impossible with God....
for He has been mindful
of the humble state of His servant....
From now on all generations
will call me blessed.*

Rights? Privileges?
Opportunities?
Ambition? Success?
*The Mighty One has done
great things for me—
holy is His name.*

❧   ❧   ❧   ❧   ❧

Considering the Challenge
"'How will this be?' Mary asked."

Feeling inadequate is a common sensation that usually accompanies our comparing ourselves with others. We can feel inadequate as mothers, as daughters, as wives, or as employees. We can also feel inadequate spiritually. Have you ever avoided opening your life up to the Lord because you doubted He would ask someone like you to serve Him in ways that you associate with more dedicated Christians? Have you thought others better equipped for the Lord's service than you? Perhaps you have compared yourself with other believers you know are devoted to serving God, such as your pastor, a missionary friend, or even some distant saint like Mother Teresa. Or you are intimidated by those who serve the Lord in less visible vocations: a young man working in a community group home for the mentally retarded, the mother of preschool children who has left a successful professional career to stay at home, or a retired couple who serve as foster grandparents to several single-parent families.

"It is not what we do that matters, *but what a sovereign*

God chooses to do through us," says Charles Colson in *Loving God.* "God doesn't want our success; He wants us. He doesn't demand our achievements; He demands our obedience." Wherever you are, whatever your job is, whether you are young or old, single or married, *God wants you.* You are His unique creation, one of a kind, with gifts and talents entrusted to your care for the purpose of bringing honor to His name. All that's required of you is a servant's heart—"May it be to me as you have said"—and you can begin serving Him where you are.

❦   ❦   ❦   ❦   ❦

Lord, in the strength of grace,
    With a glad heart and free,
Myself, my residue of days,
    I consecrate to Thee.

Thy ransomed servant, I
    restore to Thee Thy own;
And, from this moment, live or die,
    to serve my God alone.
— CHARLES WESLEY
1707-1788

❦   ❦   ❦   ❦   ❦

Putting It Into Practice
"May it be to me as you have said."

Jesus told us that "the kingdom of heaven is like a merchant looking for fine pearls. When he found one of great value, he went away and sold everything he had and bought it" (Matt. 13:45-46). Can you imagine doing such a thing? Selling *everything* you had in exchange for one item? To do so, you would have to believe that the sum total of everything you possessed was worth the price of the object. It's difficult to imagine anything being worth that kind of sacrifice!

Whether the merchant made a wise choice, writes author and psychiatrist John White, depends on whether the pearl was worth what it cost. "We see at once that treasure in heaven would be worth it," says White. "Why then are we so quick to opt for earthly treasure and so slow to be obsessed with the heavenly? Perhaps it is because *we do not believe in heavenly realities.* They represent a celestial cliché in our minds, but no more."

Accepting Christ's call to serve Him puts our money where our mouth is, demonstrating that we are choosing to believe in heavenly realities at the expense of our attachment to earthly realities. "Basically...it is *faith* that makes us step lightheartedly along the Way of the Cross—not a spirit of sacrifice but faith that the next life is important, that Jesus *is* preparing a place on high," adds Dr. White. "The Way of the Cross is a magnificent obsession with a heavenly pearl, beside which everything in life has no value. If it were a case of buying it, we would gladly sell all we had to do so."

In the parable of the merchant the emphasis is on the pearl, not on the merchant's possessions; in the kingdom of God the focus is on *the Lord Himself,* not on what we are doing on His behalf. Our actions are merely *a response to a heavenly call.*

"Whoever finds his life will lose it, and whoever loses his life for my sake will find it" (Matt. 10:39). By faith we receive God's free gift of salvation; by grace we are able to give our lives back to Him as an expression of our love for His Son.

❧   ❧   ❧   ❧   ❧

Lord, I am amazed
at Your willingness
to enter my life
   and change my heart
     and cancel my debt;
to make me part of Your body
   and send Your Spirit
     to lead me daily.

Even when I fail,
   You faithfully support
     and nourish me
    with bread

and wine
and water;
with peace
and hope
and joy.

I am thankful
for the opportunity to serve You.
It is a privilege and an honor
to be asked to join a King's household
and receive gifts to invest
on His behalf.

Strengthen me, Lord,
as I place my hope in You;
make my light shine forth
in the darkness!
I believe that Your grace is sufficient,
that Your power is made perfect
in my weakness.
Come, Holy Spirit, and make my life glow
with God's love.

❦   ❦   ❦   ❦   ❦

Points to Ponder
—THEME: *Luke 1:26-38*

My upbringing taught me to expect to grow up to be _____
_____.

Knowing that God wants me, not my success, means that I
_____
_____.

Since serving the Lord is an attitude that affects all of my relationships, my abilities, and my walk with Jesus, I can see that
_____
_____.

Serving the Lord with gladness is only possible when _____
_____
_____.

When I become tired and feel overwhelmed by what God expects of me, it helps to _____
_____.

Faith is related to serving God in the sense that _____
_____
_____.

In accordance with Hebrews 6:12, I have tried to imitate____
_____
_____.

Additional Study

— *MEDITATE ON* Psalms 90, 112, and 134.
— *READ ABOUT* two Old Testament women, Shiphrah and Puah, in Exodus 1:15-20.
— *STUDY* Matthew 25:14-30; Philippians 2:1-4; and Titus 2:11—3:8.
— *MEMORIZE* Galatians 5:13-14; Hebrews 9:14; and Psalm 34:22.

❦ ❦ ❦ ❦ ❦

Costly grace is the treasure hidden in the field; for the sake of it a man will gladly go and sell all that he has. It is the pearl of great price to buy which the merchant will sell all his goods. It is the kingly rule of Christ, for whose sake a man will pluck out the eye which causes him to stumble; it is the call of Christ at which the disciple leaves his nets and follows him. Costly grace is the gospel which must be sought again and again, the gift which must be asked for, the door at which a man must knock. Such grace is costly because it calls us to follow, and it is grace because it calls us to follow Jesus Christ.

— DIETRICH BONHOEFFER
1906-1945

ELEVEN

Laboring

*I commend to you our sister Phoebe,
a servant of the church in Cenchrea.
I ask you to receive her in the Lord
in a way worthy of the saints and to
give her any help she may need from
you, for she has been a great help to
many people, including me.*
— ROMANS 16:1

*Thank God every morning when you get
up that you have something to do which
must be done, whether you like it or not.
Being forced to work, and forced to do
your best, will breed in you temperance
and self-control, diligence and strength of
will, cheerfulness and content, and a
hundred virtues which the idle will
never know.*
— CHARLES KINGSLEY
1819-1875

*What is most rewarding is doing some-
thing that really matters with congenial
colleagues who share with us the firm
conviction that it needs to be done.*
— ELTON TRUEBLOOD

*Because we cannot see Christ, we cannot
express our love to Him in person. But
our neighbor we can see, and we can do
for him or her what we would love to do
for Jesus if He were visible.*
— MOTHER TERESA

*S*eeds and soil. Growth and harvest. These words appear often in the New Testament, providing many parallels between the fundamentals of crop raising and the process of spiritual cultivation. Discipleship involves both God's work within us and our willingness to labor within His kingdom. As believers, we see ourselves described in Scripture as both seeds and sowers, fruit and harvesters. These different and seemingly contradictory images are actually a beautiful illustration of our responsibility to both yield to God's will and to act upon it. Our Maker has created us to be productive both inside and out. Unlike labor that is aimed at food production, however, our work within the kingdom of God and His work within us yield a harvest that will endure throughout eternity.

Consider the women of the early church. We recognize the value of their labor today, nearly two thousand years later, as we read of Lydia, "a dealer in purple cloth," whose home became a meeting place for the apostles; Priscilla, a tentmaker whom Paul called "my fellow worker"; Phoebe, highlighted in a special citation for being a "servant of the church in Cenchrea"; and finally, women such as Mary, Tryphena, Tryphosa, and Persis—all commended for working "very hard in the Lord."

As women today, our work is valuable too! And like the women of the early church, we can ask ourselves, "Lord, what work would You have me be doing? How can I start to work *for You?*"

When we are born again, we choose to begin working for a new boss. Whereas our previous employer used dishonest and deceitful practices to keep us on his payroll, Jesus has promised that He will work right alongside us and will always provide us with the means to accomplish our tasks. Our Lord's management style perfectly fits who God created us to be. Thus, as we labor within His kingdom, at His direction, we receive everything we need to become productive on His behalf.

According to Dr. Roberta Hestenes, president of Eastern College in St David's, Pennsylvania, a woman who feels called by God to work in a position of ministry "should become a person of prayer and spiritual discernment, so that she really is seeking to minister out of her desire to be Christ's person and obedient to the will of God." Furthermore, Dr. Hestenes adds, "She should be willing to take risks, including the risk of not being approved of by everybody."

In thinking of the women who labored diligently for the Lord within the early church, this description seems particularly apt. They must have been women of prayer and spiritual discernment who sought to minister out of their desire to be Christ's person, obedient to God, willing to risk *everything*—including their lives—for the sake of their risen Savior. Their work mattered to God; ours can too.

There is still much to be done in God's kingdom. *We don't have to worry about unemployment when we labor for the Lord!* And He is an equal-opportunity employer, for the work of the church was never intended to be the sole preserve of men.

The New Testament clearly portrays our feminine predecessors as co-laborers with their brothers in the early church. Priscilla, Phoebe, and countless other women were hard workers who played an important part in biblical history. Acts 18:1-3, 18-26 and Romans 16:1-16 give us a glimpse of these women who became fragrant offerings as laborers within the kingdom of God.

❦ ❦ ❦ ❦ ❦

> *She has been a great help to many people,*
> *including me.*
> Phoebe!
> *Greet Priscilla and Aquila—they risked their*
> *lives for me....*
> Priscilla!
> And Mary, Junias,
> Tryphena, Tryphosa,
> Persis, Julia:
> We salute your memory!
> With few words,
> Paul left us
> a brief testimony
> of your costly contributions—
> yet we can only imagine

134

what your world
was like.
And so I picture you, Phoebe,
carrying Paul's letter
to the church in Rome,
a determined deaconess
delivering God's Word upon request,
willing to take His message
to a distant city known
for its pagan practices
and political intrigue.
And you, Priscilla—
what a remarkable woman!
Making tents with your husband,
the two of you making friends with
your fellow worker, Paul;
traveling together to Ephesus,
risking your lives
for God's chosen servant.
With strength and dignity
I imagine you toiling—and laughing—
with your companions.
Building a church
became your business, too,
an occupation worthy of the best
you had to offer,
a calling causing your deep commitment
to flower into fruitful ministry
on the Lord's behalf.

Occupation...calling...commitment...ministry.
As women today, our needs and desires are
the same:
as believers, we are seeking
to put God's love into action,
to invest our time and talents wisely,
and to learn what it means to walk
as new creatures
in a world turned upside down by sin.
There is still so much each of us can do.

135

❦ ❦ ❦ ❦ ❦

Considering the Challenge
"Those women who work hard in the Lord."

Have you found it challenging to keep your love for the Lord in focus as you work in your primary occupation? Have you been tempted to succumb to the "me first" ethic in your workplace, even as a believer? Since the early seventies it has become increasingly difficult for us as Christian women to find our identity in God's image and consequently fulfill His calling for our lives. We are pulled in a dozen different directions at once, pressured by secular role models who would have us look to a job as the source of our identity when our greatest joy as believers is meant to come from knowing and serving Christ. With few contemporary women widely recognized for their work or contributions to the church, we may miss opportunities to minister on the Lord's behalf right where we are. We may even neglect to learn from the examples God has *already* given us in His Word to teach and encourage us. But it doesn't have to be this way!

"The resolute desire of women to know, be and develop themselves, and to use their gifts in the service of the world, is so obviously God's will for them, that to deny or frustrate it is an extremely serious oppression," asserts evangelical theologian John Stott. "It is a woman's basic right and responsibility to discover herself, her identity, and her vocation.... If God endows women with spiritual gifts (which he does) and thereby calls them to exercise their gifts for the common good (which he does), then the church must recognize God's gifts and calling, must make appropriate spheres of service available to women, and should 'ordain' (that is, commission and authorize) them to exercise their God-given ministry, at least in team situations. Our Christian doctrines of creation and redemption tell us that God wants his gifted people to be fulfilled not frustrated, and his church to be enriched by their service."

In this brief passage, John Stott reaffirms the New Testament norms revealed in both the teaching of Scripture and the lives of women in the early church. As believers belonging to the church in the twentieth century, we can follow the examples of women in the Word who shared their gifts and resources with the Lord. *Like them, we are called to creatively express our womanhood through working diligently within the kingdom of God.* "Always give yourselves fully to the work of the Lord, because you know that your labor in the Lord is not in vain" (1 Cor. 15:58).

❦ ❦ ❦ ❦ ❦

If there be some weaker one,
Give me strength to help him on;
If a blinder soul there be,
Let me guide him nearer Thee.
Make my mortal dreams come true
With the work I fain would do;
Clothe with life the weak intent,
Let me be the thing I meant;
Let me find in Thine employ
Peace that dearer is than joy;
Out of self to love be led
And to heaven acclimated,
Until all things sweet and good
Seem my natural habitude.
— JOHN GREENLEAF WHITTIER
1807-1892

❦ ❦ ❦ ❦ ❦

Putting It Into Practice

"Aquila and Priscilla
greet you warmly in the Lord, and so does the church
that meets at their house."
—*1 Cor. 16:19*

"Real Christian faith is self-affirming, not self-mutilating," says Howard Snyder in *The Community of the King*. "The true Christian does not try to get rid of his self or kill his will; rather he willfully determines to do the will of the Father. True discipleship is determining to do what Jesus showed his followers must do. Love for Christ means obedience to the Jesus lifestyle."

Reading these words brings a variety of different images to mind, among them the pained expression of "self-mutilating" Christians who seem to find little or no joy in working for the Lord. But what a contrast this is to the shining faces of women who feel deeply fulfilled in their work, knowing that they are dedicating their gifts and abilities to the glory of their mighty Lord! What makes the difference? Why do some women pray and sing when they work and others usually grimace and frown? Could it be that they in some way feel obligated to work out their salvation themselves rather than rejoicing that the penalty for their sin has *already* been paid?

Snyder suggests that believers are to be "cross-bearers rather than cross-wearers" because Jesus has already paid the penalty for our sin. Bearing the cross, he writes, "does not mean simply our sicknesses and our problems and the neighbor we cannot get along with. Rather the cross means voluntarily choosing to live our lives for others, letting the life of Jesus show us what true spirituality is.... Thank God for all the benefits we receive through Jesus' death on the cross! But let us thank him also for showing us the kind of life his followers are to lead; let us thank him for his Holy Spirit, given to enable us to live the life of discipleship according to the values of the kingdom."

Remember: putting our talent and energy to use as the Lord's disciples will produce *eternal* results, whether we are missionaries in a foreign country, members of a local church ministering to the needy, teachers instructing college students, or mothers serving our families right in our own homes. God can use us effectively *wherever* He has placed us as long as we are determined to do what Jesus showed His followers must do. Laboring for the Lord is a privilege every woman may partake in with dignity and joy.

❦ ❦ ❦ ❦ ❦

Lord, help me to realize
   that I am just here momentarily,

a pilgrim passing through with work to do.
I need to know that
You are right here with me
as I work—that You are
my strength,
my life, and
my comfort.
I thank You
for being
my *daily bread,*
my *living water,*
and my *faithful Shepherd!*
Give me the courage and the know-how to labor
diligently for You
and show me how to use
my time here wisely,
to Your honor and glory.

❧ ❧ ❧ ❧ ❧

Points to Ponder
—THEME: *Acts 18:1-3, 18-26 and Romans 16:1-16*

I am confident that God has called me to work for Him by using my ability to _____
_____.

Because my identity is rooted in who I am in Christ rather than in what I do, laboring for Him can never be a substitute for _____
_____.

As a woman, my work within God's kingdom is to be _____
_____
_____.

At this point in my life my primary focus of ministry appears to be _____
_____.

If I were to make out a list of my "job responsibilities" according to the work God calls His people to do, it would include _____
_____.

I could better invest and use my resources—talents, finances, energy, knowledge—if _____
_____
_____.

On days when I feel unappreciated or unrecognized for the work I do, I _____
_____.

Additional Study
— *MEDITATE ON* Psalms 41:1-3, 113, and 146.
— *READ ABOUT* an Old Testament woman, possibly Solomon's mother, Bathsheba, in Proverbs 31:10-31.
— *STUDY* Matthew 25:31-46; Galatians 6:7-10; and Hebrews 6:10-12.
— *MEMORIZE* Proverbs 14:21; Colossians 3:23, 24; and 19:17.

❧ ❧ ❧ ❧ ❧

I am glad to think
I am not bound to make the world go right, But
only to discover and to do
With cheerful heart the work that God appoints.

I will trust him
That he can hold his own; and I will take
His will, above the work he sendeth me,
To be my chiefest good.
                    —*JEAN INGELOW*
                    1820-1897

TWELVE

Proclaiming

*So the women hurried away...afraid, yet
filled with joy, and ran to tell his disciples.*
—MATTHEW 28:8

*I am obliged to bear witness because I hold
a particle of light, and to keep it to myself
would be equivalent to extinguishing it.*
— GABRIEL MARCEL

*The Company of Jesus is not people
streaming to a shrine; and it is not people
making up an audience for a speaker; it is
laborers engaged in the harvesting task
of reaching their perplexed and seeking
brethren with something so vital that,
if it is received, it will change their lives.*
— ELTON TRUEBLOOD

Consider the qualities of light in comparison to darkness: light creates color, brightens nature, reveals our environment, and illuminates the heavens. Darkness erases visibility altogether. Light vividly separates each hue into a finite position on the color spectrum. Darkness paints our world in fuzzy shades of gray. Light exposes things for what they are, placing reality in its proper perspective. Darkness hides it all, telling us nothing whatsoever about our surroundings.

"I am the light of the world," declares Jesus to a world shrouded in sin. "Whoever follows me will never walk in darkness, but will have the light of life" (John 8:12). The Son of God has promised to brighten every corner of our lives with the revealing light of His truth. He tells us that if we live by His truth, we will come "into the light," so that everything we do is seen plainly (John 3:21). It is as if we are sitting in a master photographer's studio— nothing is hidden from view! Our lower nature rebels against this type of "exposure." (Who wants to have her picture taken when every enlarged pore, stray hair, and unsightly blemish will be seen?) Yet even as His light reveals, His grace heals. The more we *know about* Jesus' love, the less we feel like hiding. Eventually we learn to thank our Redeemer for everything His light brings into focus.

The light of Christ is not limited to this dimension of life only, however. "*You* are the light of the world," Jesus announces to those of us who are believers. Think of it: we have not only been *personally touched* by the light of Christ—we are actually *bearers* of that light! Isn't it incredible to think that we carry His light with us wherever we go? "For you were once darkness, but now you are light in the Lord" (Eph. 5:8).

Peter wrote that as people of God we are "to proclaim the triumphs of him who has called you out of the darkness into his marvelous light" (1 Peter 2:9 NEB). By proclaiming Jesus Christ as Lord and Savior and finding our identity in His image, we need no longer fear His light; rather, we can rejoice in it! In Matthew 28:1-10 and John 20:10-18 we see the earliest scenes of those who were sent to proclaim Christ's victorious triumph over the grave. As you reflect on these passages, celebrate the wonder of what Jesus has done and

continues to do in women's lives as we become fragrant
offerings for the glory of God.

❦   ❦   ❦   ❦   ❦

So the women hurried away from the tomb,
    afraid yet filled with joy,
and ran to tell the disciples,
    "We have seen the Lord!"

They were still running,
    breathless and bursting with energy,
when they hit the door.

Can you imagine?
Footsteps interspersed with alleluias
    all the way into town—
and then the incredible announcement:
    "We have seen the Lord!"
            And yet,
the news
    is just as magnificent
        today,
            isn't it?

You turned
    my wailing into dancing;
You removed
    my sackcloth and clothed me with joy,
that my heart may sing
    to You and not be silent.
O Lord, my God, I will give You thanks forever!

❦   ❦   ❦   ❦   ❦

Considering the Challenge
    "The women hurried away from the tomb,
            afraid yet filled with joy."

Have you discovered the joy of proclaiming the news of

Christ's victory to others? Have you realized that God wants to *use you* to tell others about His Son?

"My heart is full of Christ, and longs its glorious matter to declare!" wrote Charles Wesley, expressing the cry of every believer who has come to know the reality of what Jesus has done. Like Mary of Magdala, we have turned away from the tomb and want to bear witness to the triumph of our Lord.

"The evidence of the gospel is not primarily in some document but in the lives of Christ's followers," asserts Elton Trueblood in *The Company of the Committed*. "We do not have to wait until we know the whole truth...to make our witness. If we were to wait for this, we should wait forever.... It was the vocation of Christ to bear witness to the truth; it is our vocation to bear witness to Him."

But how do we best accomplish this?

According to Trueblood, "The best way to reach another life is by saying, as simply as possible, 'Whereas I was blind, but now I see.'... The value of the individual story of Christ's healing power lies largely in the undeniable fact that each human life stands at a unique point in the total web of human experience, and, as a consequence, each one has an approach to others which is not identical with the opportunity of any other human being.... The worker on the production line may have an entree to the life of his fellow worker on the line that can never be matched by any pastor or teacher or professional evangelist. The responsiblity of each individual Christian is to do that which no other person can do as well as he can."

For Mary of Magdala and the women of Galilee the opportunity to proclaim the news of Christ's resurrection was a spectacular occasion that placed them at a unique position in the web of history. Nearly two thousand years later, God is calling each one of us to bear witness to our beloved Savior and Lord in our world.

❦   ❦   ❦   ❦   ❦

I said, "Let me walk in the fields."
He said, "No, walk in the town."

145

I said, "There are no flowers there."
   He said, "No flowers, but a crown."

I said, "But the skies are black;
   There is nothing but noise and din."
And He wept as He sent me back;
   "There is more," He said, "there is sin."

I said, "But the air is thick,
   And fogs are veiling the sun."
He answered, "Yet souls are sick,
   And souls in the dark undone."

I said, "I shall miss the light,
   And friends will miss me, they say."
He answered, "Choose to-night
   If I am to miss you, or they."

I pleaded for time to be given.
   He said, "Is it hard to decide?
It will not seem hard in heaven
   To have followed the steps of your Guide."

I cast one look at the fields,
   Then set my face to the town;
He said, "My child, do you yield?
   Will you leave the flowers for the crown?"

Then into His hand went mine,
   And into my heart came He;
And I walk in a light divine
   The path I had feared to see.
             — GEORGE MACDONALD

        ❦   ❦   ❦   ❦   ❦

Putting It Into Practice
      "Go quickly and tell...."

"Isn't it interesting," says Charles Colson, "that Jesus didn't set up an office in the temple and wait for people to come to Him for counseling? Instead, He went to them—to the homes of the most notorious sinners, to the places where He would most likely encounter the handicapped and the sick, the needy, the outcasts of society.... *Taking the gospel to people wherever they are*—death row, the ghetto, or next door—*is frontline evangelism.* Frontline love. *It is our one hope for breaking down barriers and for restoring the sense of community, of caring for one another,* that our decadent, impersonalized culture has sucked out of us."

The life function of the church, continues Colson, "is to love the God who created it—to care for others out of obedience to Christ, to heal those who are hurt, to take away fear, to restore community, to belong to one another, to proclaim the Good News while living it out. The church is the invisible made visible.... Our presence in a place of need is more powerful than a thousand sermons. *Being there* is our witness."

Yet, as George MacDonald's poem beautifully illustrates, it is often difficult for us to go to the places where the need for Christ is the greatest. It takes courage and time and effort. Perhaps He is telling you to quit a job you love and stay home and raise children; perhaps He is asking you to work in a crisis pregnancy center or a shelter for abused and battered women; or perhaps he is calling you to minister to the elderly in a local nursing home. Proclaiming His love often requires a sacrifice of our personal ease.

"You are the world's light....Don't hide your light! Let it shine for all; let your good deeds glow for all to see, so that they may praise your heavenly Father" (Matt. 5:14-16 LB). Jesus proclaimed these words from a hilltop, not a sanctuary, dressed in simple garments, not priestly robes.

We live in a dark world filled with lonely and troubled and hurting people. As a woman of God, are you like a city on a hill, glowing in the night with His light, for all to see?

❦ ❦ ❦ ❦ ❦

Lord, from the heights of heaven
    You descended into human flesh
        to bring the light of Your life
            to me.
You opened my eyes to realms of glory
    through a Cross,
announcing *pardon* and *hope*,
    freedom and *forgiveness*
        to all who believe.
Jesus, I thank You!

Shine through me, Lord,
    as I proclaim Your victory
        and bear witness to Your love.
I rejoice in Your gift to me!
I place my life in Your hands!

❧   ❧   ❧   ❧   ❧

Points to Ponder
—THEME: *Matthew 28:1-10 and John 20:10-18*

Telling others what the Lord has done in my life is _____
_____
_____.

I have missed the chance to share my faith with others when
_____
_____.

Witnessing to people around me comes about more naturally
if I _____
_____.

Jesus refers to His followers as the light of the world because
_____
_____.

I have seen the success of Christian witness in an unlikely setting when _____
_____.

It is difficult to go to the places where the need for Christ is
the greatest because _____
_____.

Additional Study

— *MEDITATE ON* Psalms 9, 18:28-36, and 22:22-31.
— *READ ABOUT* an Old Testment woman, Queen Esther, in Esther 4:4—5:8 and 7:1— 8:17.
— *STUDY* Ephesians 5:8-14; Philippians 2:14-16, 3:7-21; 1 John 1:5-7; and Psalms 34:1-5 and 37:5-6.
— *MEMORIZE* John 3:20-21 and Proverbs 4:18.

❧　❧　❧　❧　❧

May 7, 1838. This morning I left Leamington for Bristol. I had grace to confess the Lord Jesus the last part of the way before several merry passengers, and had the honour of being ridiculed for His sake. There are few things in which I feel more entirely dependent upon the Lord, than in confessing Him on such occasions. Sometimes I have, by grace, had much real boldness; but often I have shown the greatest weakness, doing no more than refraining entirely from unholy conversation, without speaking a single word for Him who toiled beyond measure for me.

No other remedy do I know for myself and any of my fellow-saints who are weak, like myself, in this respect, than to seek to have the heart so full of Jesus, and to live so in the realisation of what He has done for us, that without any effort, out of the full heart, we may speak for Him.

—GEORGE MÜLLER

Reaching

It is not to be thought that I have already achieved all this. I have not yet reached perfection, but I press on, hoping to take hold of that for which Christ once took hold of me. My friends, I do not reckon myself to have got hold of it yet. All I can say is this: forgetting what is behind me, and reaching out for what lies ahead, I press toward the goal to win the prize which is God's call to the life above, in Christ Jesus.

—PHILIPPIANS 3:12-14 NEB

Naturally, we care not about the holiness
of God. Naturally, man likes to please
himself, and would have God be like
himself. The attribute of holiness is the
last, naturally, we care about. But when
we are born again, when we are renewed,
when we have spiritual life, there is born
in our hearts a longing after holiness,
and we rejoice in the fact that God is a
holy Being.
— GEORGE MÜLLER

Godliness means responding to God's
revelation in trust and obedience, faith
and worship, prayer and praise,
submission and service. Life must be seen
and lived in the light of God's Word.
This, and nothing else, is true religion.
— J.I. PACKER

As women who have been transformed by the light of Christ, we place our hope in the same Lord who defended Mary of Bethany and appeared on Easter morning to the women from Galilee. As believers who have found our identity in the character and image of God, we trust in the One who knows the condition of our hearts, the One who is "the same yesterday and today and forever" (Heb. 13:8).

Are you trusting Him today? Can you believe that He is bringing you ever closer to being conformed to the image of His precious Son? *God's call to the life above, in Christ Jesus.* We can live in hopeful expectation of that day knowing that He will not abandon the work He has begun.

"Yes, Lord, I trust You! Heavenly Father, I believe that You are conforming me to the image of Your Son!"

❧ ❧ ❧ ❧ ❧

In the still air the music lies unheard;
In the rough marble beauty lies unseen:
To make the music and the beauty, needs
The master's touch, the sculptor's chisel
keen.

Great Master, touch us with Thy skillful hand;
Let not the music that is within us die!
Great Sculptor, hew and polish us; nor let,
Hidden and lost, Thy form within us lie!

Spare not the stroke! do with us as Thou wilt!
Let there naught be unfinished, broken,
marred;
Complete Thy purpose, that we may become
Thy perfect image, Thou our God and Lord!
— HORATIUS BONAR

❧ ❧ ❧ ❧ ❧

To make the music and the beauty
   needs the master's touch
      and the sculptor's chisel keen....
Yes, Lord!
 Make Your music ring in our hearts;
bring forth Your beauty
   through the offering of our lives
      as we place ourselves in Your hands.
Fashion us according to Your purposes.
Teach us what it means
   to live by grace
      and overflow with thankfulness
         as You mold and shape us at Your will.
Give us the courage to be women
   worthy of bearing Your name
      as we are
becoming
   choosing
      turning
         walking
            abiding
               seeking
                  praying
                     praising
                        sharing
                           serving
                             laboring
                                proclaiming!

Praise be to the God and Father of our
   Lord Jesus Christ!
In His great mercy He has given us
   new birth into a living hope
      through the resurrection of Jesus from
        the dead,
   and into an inheritance that can never
      perish,
         spoil
            or fade—
kept in heaven for you, who through faith

are shielded by God's power until
the coming of salvation that is ready to
be revealed in the last time.

New birth into a *living hope!*
An inheritance that can never
  perish,
    spoil
      or fade—
      kept in heaven
      for us!

❦   ❦   ❦   ❦   ❦

Let your heart rejoice in these words as you place them securely in its inner chambers. Be encouraged by the promises of God, who shields us by His power as we await the coming of the Lord.

Like clay on the potter's wheel, do not wonder why you are being shaped and molded as your life conforms to the shape of the Master's hands. Simply yield, and one day you will find that He has transformed you into a flawless masterpiece fit to spend eternity in His glorious Presence.

"Therefore," wrote the apostle Peter, "prepare your minds for action; be self-controlled; set your hope fully on the grace to be given to you when Jesus Christ is revealed" (1 Peter 1:13). No other hope but Jesus. No other goal but "the prize which is God's call to the life above, in Christ Jesus."

And so we will be with the Lord forever.
Therefore encourage one another with these words.
—1 Thessalonians 4:18

❦   ❦   ❦   ❦   ❦

Let patience have her perfect work. Statue under the chisel of the sculptor, stand steady to the blows of his mallet. Clay on the wheel, let the fingers of the divine potter mold you at their will. Obey the Father's lightest word: hear the Brother who knows you and died for you.

—GEORGE MACDONALD

Bibliography

Bonhoeffer, Dietrich. *The Cost of Discipleship*. New York: Macmillan, 1963.

Bridges, Jerry. *The Pursuit of Holiness*. Colorado Springs: NavPress, 1978.

Bunyan, John. *Pilgrim's Prayer Book*. Louis Gifford Parkhurst, Jr., ed. Wheaton, Ill.: Tyndale House, 1986.

Carmichael, Amy. *Whispers of Hope*. Old Tappan, N.J.: Fleming H. Revell, 1982.

Chambers, Oswald. *My Utmost for His Highest*. New York: Dodd, Mead & Co., 1935.

Cole, C. Donald. *Thirsting for God: A Devotional Study of the Psalms*. Westchester, Ill.: Crossway Books, 1986.

Colson, Charles. *Loving God*. Grand Rapids, Mich.: Zondervan Publishing House, 1983.

Dillard, Annie. *Pilgrim at Tinker Creek*. New York: Harper & Row, 1985.

Gordon, S.D. *Quiet Talks on Prayer*. Westwood, N.J.: The Christian Library, 1984.

Heald, Cynthia. *Becoming a Woman of Excellence*. Colorado Springs: NavPress, 1986.

Hurnard, Hannah. *Hind's Feet on High Places*. Wheaton, Ill.: Tyndale House, 1977.

Hymns for the Family of God. Nashville: Paragon Music, 1978.

Keyes, Dick. *Beyond Identity: Finding Your Self in the Character and Image of God.* Ann Arbor, Mich.: Servant Books, 1984.

Lawrence, Brother. *The Practice of the Presence of God.* Edited by Donald E. Demaray. Grand Rapids, Mich.: Baker Book House, 1975.

Lewis, C.S. *George MacDonald: An Anthology.* New York: Macmillan, 1946.

_____. *Mere Christianity.* New York: Macmillan, 1960.

Lloyd-Jones, D. Martyn. *The Cross.* Westchester, Ill.: Crossway Books, 1986.

MacDonald, George. *Creation in Christ.* Edited by Rolland Hein. Wheaton, Ill.: Harold Shaw Publishers, 1976.

Morrison, James Dalton, ed. *Masterpieces of Religious Verse.* Grand Rapids, Mich.: Baker Book House, 1977.

Müller, George. *The George Müller Treasury.* Edited by Roger Steer. Westchester, Ill.: Crossway Books, 1986.

Murray, Andrew. *Abide in Christ.* Old Tappan, N.J.: Fleming H. Revell/Spire Books.

Ortlund, Anne. *Disciplines of the Beautiful Woman.* Waco, Tex.: Word Books, 1977.

Packer, J.I. *Knowing God.* Downers Grove, Ill.: InterVarsity Press, 1973.

Peterson, Eugene. *Earth and Altar.* Downers Grove, Ill.: InterVarsity Press, 1985.

Schaeffer, Edith. *A Way of Seeing.* Old Tappan, N.J.: Fleming H. Revell, 1977.

Schaeffer, Francis. *The Mark of a Christian.* Downers Grove, Ill.: InterVarsity Press, 1970.

_____. *True Spirituality.* Downers Grove, Ill.: InterVarsity Press, 1971.

Smith, Hannah Whitall. *The Christian's Secret of a Happy Life.* Old Tappan, N.J.: Fleming H. Revell/Spire Books, 1970.

Snyder, Howard. *The Community of the King.* Downers Grove, Ill.: InterVarsity Press, 1977.

Stafford, Tim. *Knowing the Face of God.* Grand Rapids, Mich.: Zondervan Publishing House, 1986.

Stott, John R.W. *Involvement: Social and Sexual Relationships in the Modern World.* Vol. 2. Old Tappan,

N.J.: Fleming H. Revell, 1985.

Torrey, R.A. *How to Pray.* Old Tappan, N.J.: Fleming H. Revell, 1900.

Tozer, A.W. *The Knowledge of the Holy.* New York: Harper & Row/Jubilee, 1975.

Trueblood, D. Elton. *The Company of the Committed.* New York: Harper & Row, 1961.

Tucker, Ruth and Liefeld, Walter. *Daughters of the Church,* Grand Rapids, Mich.: Zondervan, 1987.

White, John. *The Cost of Commitment.* Downers Grove, Ill.: InterVarsity Press, 1976.

_____ . *Flirting with the World.* Downers Grove, Ill.: InterVarsity Press, 1983.

Wiersbe, Warren. *Real Worship.* Nashville: Oliver-Nelson, 1986.

Wilson, Earl. *The Undivided Self.* Downers Grove, Ill.: InterVarsity Press, 1983.

Wirt, Sherwood Eliot, ed. *Spiritual Awakening.* Westchester, Ill.: Crossway Books, 1986.

_____. *Spiritual Disciplines.* Westchester, Ill.: Crossway Books, 1983 (March).

Yancey, Philip. "The Shape of God's Body." *Leadership,* Summer 1987, Vol. VIII, No. 3, pp. 88-94.